The Entrepreneurial Investor

THE ART, SCIENCE, AND BUSINESS OF VALUE INVESTING

Paul Orfalea
Lance Helfert
Atticus Lowe
Dean Zatkowsky

John Wiley & Sons, Inc.

Published by John Wiley & Sons, Inc., Hoboken, New Jersey.
Published simultaneously in Canada.

Wiley Bicentennial Logo: Richard J. Pacifico

For general information on our other products and services or for technical support, please contact our Customer Care Department within the United States at (800) 762-2974, outside the United States at (317) 572-3993 or fax (317) 572-4002.

Wiley also publishes its books in a variety of electronic formats. Some content that appears in print may not be available in electronic formats. For more information about Wiley products, visit our Web site at www.wiley.com.

Library of Congress Cataloging-in-Publication Data:

The entrepreneurial investor : the art, science, and business of value investing / Paul Orfalea ... [et al.].
　　　p. cm.
　Includes index.
　ISBN 978-0-470-22714-5 (cloth)
　1. Stocks. 2. Value investing. 3. Investment analysis. 4. Corporations–Valuation.
I. Orfalea, Paul.
　HG4661.E58 2008
　332.67'8–dc22
　　　　　　　　　　　　　　2007034468
Printed in the United States of America

10 9 8 7 6 5 4 3 2 1

Contents

Foreword

A HOW-TO BOOK FROM PEOPLE WHO REALLY KNOW HOW TO

Let me tell you why this business book is different right from the start. It's written by people who know what they're talking about. Now I know what you're thinking—aren't all business books written by people who should know what they're talking about?

Well, yes, they *should* be. But, sadly, they are not. Whole forests of trees have been wasted on investment and financial missives written by experts who were neither experts nor remotely capable of offering advice. It's like the old gag about guys driving to Wall Street in Rolls-Royces so they can get advice from guys who take the subway to work. Or the guy who goes to a financial planner's house, only to discover he lives in a dump. How good a financial planner could he be?

I don't know for sure about Paul's home, but something tells me it's not a dump. His rags-to-riches, true Horatio Alger story is now the stuff of business legend. Far from lamenting his academic challenges, he joked about them. He turned his weaknesses into his strengths. He joked about his dyslexic brain. He also built an empire called Kinko's, despite the doubters and the cynics and all those smart kids who, no doubt, dismissed him.

The difference was, and is, that Paul didn't dismiss himself and learned not to casually dismiss others. Paul's entrepreneurial vision and gut-level commitment to his coworkers' welfare make him a powerful magnet for talent, as we saw first at Kinko's, and now at West Coast Asset Management. You see, Paul's keen understanding of business comes from his deeper understanding that companies are made of people. His appreciation for the talents of others made him and many of his Kinko's coworkers rich. His gut is right again with this book on the West Coast Asset Management approach to investing. He and his coauthors teach with clarity and wit and, yes, warmth.

You see, what separates Paul Orfalea from so many of the hotshot money types I've interviewed over these many years is that he cares and he relates. He knows what it's like to be on the wrong side of the tracks, on the wrong side of education, and on the wrong side of life. He knows what it's like to be passed over and forgotten, ridiculed, and ignored. And no matter the money or fame or attention he's deservedly gotten since, he always remembers those beginnings. I like to think of my friend Paul as the rock star who never forgot the day when he was just a fan, just another slug trying to make it. He's a rock star who approaches fans with a super real smile and super firm handshake and super laser-like eye contact.

In a sense, Paul is still the revolutionary entrepreneur he always was—sensing needs, exploiting opportunities, profiting where others fear to tread. The difference now, with this book, is that he's letting us in on his secrets. The fact that this book doesn't go on and on tells you something about Paul and his coauthors. They don't waste time babbling. They make time *informing*. The number of words doesn't determine a book's success; the *choice* of those words makes the difference. Small as this book is, it carries considerable weight.

Paul, Lance, Atticus, and Dean know that investing, like starting a business, requires an experienced gut as well as a disciplined brain. It's a pity that very smart money managers to this day don't get that. They serve their clients miserably. As guests on financial television shows, they serve their viewers even more miserably. I am most angered as a business journalist and executive when it becomes clear that the experts I'm interviewing aren't really experts at all. They hide behind lofty titles and degrees, but fail to show even the remotest form of common sense.

Paul and his team say in few words what legions of so-called Wall Street brainiacs have tried in endless volumes. Only these guys do it with flare and wit and real-life success.

Frankly, I think it is the greatest of sins that those who make it rarely share their experiences so that others can make it, too. West Coast Asset Management's services may be available only to the rich, but here we can all learn their investing philosophy, how they evaluate the quality of a company, how they read financial statements, and how they distinguish between the value and the price of a prospective investment. Once again, Paul Orfalea has built a company where people are eager to share their success.

These guys share. These guys teach. These guys care. Between them, Lance, Atticus, and Dean have worked with Paul for over 35 years. These four share a strong belief that success comes from values, not valuables.

And that is the ultimate triumph of this book. I know they're talking about ways you can understand the value of an investment. But I also know they want to leave you talking about the value of something else—life and learning, and enriching yourself as well as your wallet.

It is fitting that a man who built his fortune a nickel at a time has learned a great deal about the value of money and the values that build successful companies. *The Entrepreneurial Investor* applies those lessons to the art of investing.

Read it. Discuss it. And, like Paul and his coworkers, live it.

NEIL CAVUTO
Anchor and Sr. Vice President
Fox News Channel and Fox Business Channel

Introduction

IS INVESTING AN ART OR A SCIENCE?

Business bookshelves overflow with titles promising formulas for success in the stock market. It makes one wonder why everyone is not yet wealthy. Could it be that there is no magic formula? Could it be that investing well requires talent, education, and hard work?

Unfortunately, the answer is yes, no, and maybe. You may be able to work many hours of each day, but your money and your ideas can work 24 hours a day, 7 days a week, and they should. Wealth accrues to people who know how to make money while they read, watch television, eat, drink, work, and yes, even while they sleep. Investing through the stock market is one way to do this, and it is our passion and our business.

When people ask whether we believe investing is an art or a science, they usually intend *art* and *science* to represent "intuition" and "knowledge," respectively. So the real question is this: If we studied hard enough and executed the formula precisely, could we always make profitable choices? Or does investing require high levels of talent, sensitivity, and intuition, such that only a gifted few can prosper?

These questions have little to do with entrepreneurial investing, but since many authors and financial advisers propagate the illusion that investing is a science, the subject merits further discussion. Let us begin by stating plainly that investing is not a science, although investors should behave like scientists. Further, investing is not an art per se, but certain artistic sensibilities improve one's chance of success. In fact, the traits common to artists and scientists also help investors: keen observation, active imagination, courage to experiment, and openness to change.

Proof that Investing Is Not a Science

Consider the scientific method: we observe phenomena, imagine hypotheses, test those hypotheses through experimentation, and refine our hypotheses based on results. The objective is a consistently replicable finding.

Thus, we may dispense with the notion that investing is a science by quoting the words that appear on nearly every piece of literature issued by the investment community: "Past performance is no guarantee of future results." Science depends on replication of results; even the best investors cannot consistently replicate results, and therefore, investing is not a science.

Obsession with Charts and Graphs Does Not Equal Science

Many brokers, analysts, and other professionals rely on statistical analyses and tools like Monte Carlo simulators (a highly sophisticated computer model that accounts for thousands of variables to predict the future value of a portfolio). Despite these obsessive forms of measurement and projection, they still must concede that past performance is no guarantee of future results. We're not taking cheap shots at our colleagues—we use a wide range of analytical tools as well, but we harbor no illusions that these tools provide answers. Rather, we use them to sharpen our questions.

Mechanical Replacements for Management

Some people feel they must have an answer for everything, and they cannot bear ambiguity. They craft elaborate mechanisms to bring "order" to a very complex marketplace. Many depend on mechanical trading rules and stop loss orders, that is, automatically selling a stock if the value drops by a predetermined amount.

All have reams of data and powerful computer models to support their beliefs. These "scientific" approaches are designed to minimize management bias and human error, but they also serve to reduce individual accountability. And they rarely achieve their goals.

Investing Requires the Exercise of Human Judgment

An entrepreneurial investor weighs available information, determines whether a stock is a good buy, and then manages the investment. For example, if we buy a stock priced at $80 because we believe its actual value is really $140, we also understand that the stock might drop to $60 in the short term. All else being equal, if we liked the stock at $80 we should *love* it at $60, so we buy more because it is an even better deal. Someone with an automatic sell rule would simply take the loss and miss the long-term gains. As Warren Buffett's mentor Benjamin Graham said, "In the short term the stock market is a voting machine, but in the long run it is a weighing machine." Over time, one's opinion (vote) matters less than the actual value (weight) of a company. Hold that thought, because it is central to the tenets of entrepreneurial investing.

Much of Wall Street focuses on price-to-earnings ratios (P/Es) and future growth estimates. They often do not account for debt and tangible assets as we might. Individual investors, however, often act on hunches, letting their feelings interfere with reason. Approaches that do not respect the balance of art and science can miss opportunities and destroy capital.

For example, a company with a P/E of 20 and significant debt is much riskier than a company with a P/E of 20 and net tangible assets (value of real assets that can be sold, such as real estate, marketable securities, and cash) worth 50 percent of the company's current share price, all other things being equal. The funny thing about this is that a company with valuable real estate may understate earnings due to the depreciation of its real estate assets, so the P/E figure itself becomes less meaningful. Scientists applying formulas often miss this connection, making superficial decisions based on irrelevant information. An entrepreneurial investor, however, artfully seeks to understand the business and the meaning of its price.

Artists, Scientists, and Businesspeople

Entrepreneurs are often accused of operating too intuitively, relying more on their gut than their data. But as the saying goes, "Data is not information, information is not knowledge, and knowledge is not wisdom." Experience refines one's judgment beyond the mere collecting of facts. To improve investment results, entrepreneurial investors behave like scientists and artists, using tools and traits refined over years of practice. But are we practicing an art or a science? Perhaps neither. An entrepreneurial investor views investing as *business*, a noble discipline with its own craft, conventions, and aesthetics.

It is our belief that success or failure in equity investing depends on your ability to think and behave like a business owner. In other words, even if you have never owned your own business, entrepreneurial thinking will make you a better investor.

Ultimately, investing in stock gives you benefits of ownership without many of the headaches. But the likelihood of outstanding returns improves when you treat investing itself as a business. Thus, entrepreneurial investing operates on two levels: (1) managing your investments as if investing were your business, and (2) acting as if the companies in which you invest belong to you lock, stock, and barrel.

This is simpler than it sounds. In fact, this book is an argument for simplicity in your approach to investing. Some Wall Street firms work very hard to overcomplicate and dramatize investing. We think there is a better way for people to approach the stock market, and it starts with an understanding of this fundamental concept: The stock market is, in fact, just a market. We believe that *what* you buy—and why you buy it—matters more than *where* you buy it. But "the market" still matters because it influences prices. We focus on individual companies so we can understand whether they are undervalued by the market. This simple idea animates West Coast Asset Management's entrepreneurial investing style.

In late 2000, Lance Helfert and Kinko's founder Paul Orfalea decided to pool their years of investing experience and share their expertise with a select group of high-net-worth individuals and institutions. They launched West Coast Asset Management (WCAM), serving six clients and managing approximately $25 million in assets. In June 2007, as we finalized this manuscript for publication, WCAM had grown to a company of eleven coworkers, managing $522 million for over one hundred clients. In less than six years, WCAM grew almost five times as large as the average asset manager in the United States, according to statistics from National Regulatory Services. In February 2006, WCAM also launched the West Coast Opportunity Fund LLC (available exclusively to accredited investors), and serves as managing member.

What accounts for this growth? Nearly all of our new clients come from referrals because we do very little outside promotion or advertising. We believe the growth can be attributed to our performance and the attraction of our unique entrepreneurial investing style. By themselves, the primary characteristics of entrepreneurial investing are not unique among professional investors or business owners:

Focused: We invest in a highly concentrated portfolio of companies we thoroughly understand. This is unusual, but not unique. Warren Buffett could make the same claim.

Opportunistic: We will consider any publicly traded company, with no limitations on size or industry, and although we invest for the long term, we remain flexible so we can act nimbly when new opportunities arise. "Go-anywhere" or "all-cap" managers are still fairly rare, but again, not unique.

Involved: We conduct our own hands-on research to better understand the companies in which we invest, and we personally invest in the same companies we choose for our clients. Moreover, we approach every investment as if we were buying the entire company for ourselves. These features are surprisingly uncommon.

Individually, these traits may not be unique, but together they comprise an investing style that has proven unusually powerful and resilient. Seeking to describe the style, we realized that these characteristics describe the same focus, opportunism, and involvement we attribute to successful entrepreneurs.

A quotation from Benjamin Graham, the father of value investing and Warren Buffett's mentor, provided the icing on the cake: "Investing is most intelligent when it is most businesslike." Exactly! *Entrepreneurial investing applies the best practices of business to the business of investing!* Sure, it sounds obvious, but as we said above, much of the financial "services" industry devotes itself to obfuscation of this simple concept: Buying stock means taking ownership of a company. Always know what you are buying and why.

Is This Book a How-To, or a Who-To?

To invest with anything less than total commitment to a businesslike approach is to step into the realm of speculation and gambling. And therein lies the unfortunate irony of this book: Once we describe how to be an entrepreneurial investor, you will see that successful investing is very easy to understand but can be very difficult to execute.

Or, as we often say, entrepreneurial investing is simple but not easy.

As simple as the concepts are, most people lack the time, temperament, and talent to manage investments in the entrepreneurial style. For those few who do have the time, the patience, and the education or experience to manage their own investments, this book provides a window into how we operate and how an entrepreneurial investor benefits from focus, opportunism, and involvement.

For the large number of investors and prospective investors who depend on others to guide decisions, this book will help you understand fundamental investing concepts so you may choose a manager whose philosophy and strategy are a good fit with your own.

Fortune Cookie Wisdom

Since March 2001, we have published our *Exclusive Outlook* newsletter to help demystify the art of investing. We share concepts that can help you become a better investor, whether you choose your own stocks or hire someone to manage your investments. Like *Exclusive Outlook*, this book is not about which stocks to buy, but the ownership mind-set, explored through four parts:

1. **Think like an Owner: The Art of the Entrepreneurial Investor** covers our investing philosophy and some of the context and chatter that can cloud one's thinking.
2. **Companies Worth Owning** discusses the heart of entrepreneurial investing: choosing to invest in individual companies rather than in mutual funds or "the market."
3. **The Owner's Manual** covers some of the essential information available to prospective investors, from the advice shouted on television to annual reports, financial statements, and the ever mysterious subject of inventory.
4. **What's It Worth—To *Me?*** This section distinguishes investing from speculating. If you understand the actual *value* of a company, you then also know when the *price* is low enough for buying or high enough for selling. After all, two of the most important questions an owner must ask are these: (1) How does this company make money? and (2) How does this company make money for *me?*

Years ago, Paul Orfalea opened a fortune cookie that read, "Your eyes believe what they see. Your ears believe others." This perfectly describes the entrepreneurial approach to business and investing: a do-it-yourself sensibility based on following the facts, not the fads.

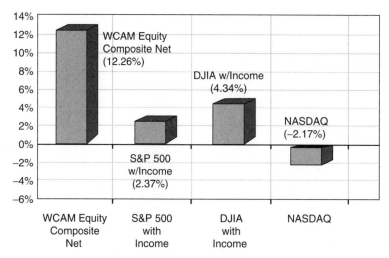

**Figure I.1   WCAM Annualized Performance, Net of Fees
(January 31, 2001–March 31, 2007)**

See complete GIPS disclosures in the Notes & Disclosures section.

Visit www.wcam.com for up-to-date performance information.

That fortune cookie's message should resonate with the hands-on sensibility of entrepreneurs everywhere. As we describe our investing philosophy (see Figure I.1) and process in the following pages, we hope *The Entrepreneurial Investor* will inspire you to treat investing like a business, and to think of yourself as the owner, because when making money *is* your business, business is good indeed.

Overview

Part One: Think like an Owner:
The Art of the Entrepreneurial Investor

How is an entrepreneurial investor different from any other type of investor? This section describes the philosophy, investing style, and attitudes toward Wall Street that distinguish the entrepreneurial investor.

1. Eyes Believe What They See; Ears Believe Others.

We've been trained to doubt ourselves, thanks to the advice of experts. Learn to trust your own judgment, and how to evaluate the advice of others.

2. Others' Irrationality Is Your Opportunity.

In most arenas, cool heads prevail. People bemoan market volatility, but volatility creates opportunity for alert investors. A long-term view empowers short-term opportunistic flexibility.

3. Dirty Harry's Investment Philosophy.

"Do you feel lucky, punk?" is not a good investing philosophy. "A man's got to know his limitations," said an older and wiser Inspector Callahan, and we agree. Staying within one's circle of competence, an entrepreneurial investor reduces the influence of luck—and ignorance.

4. Adversity in Diversity: Portfolio Concentration.

Diversification is widely misunderstood. Risk-indifferent investors underdiversify. Risk-averse investors overdiversify. Entrepreneurial investors diversify enough to mitigate unsystematic risk (company-specific risk), but concentrate for stronger returns.

5. Just Buy the Best (Which Does Not Include Most Mutual Funds).

An entrepreneurial investor's opportunistic nature leads to what the financial press has dubbed a "go-anywhere" style. Avoid constraints and limitations in the form of "style boxes" and other financial services marketing tools. Opportunity doesn't fit in a box.

6. Inspirational Figures: Benjamin Graham.

Lessons from the father of value investing are as valuable today as when he wrote *Security Analysis* with David Dodd in 1934.

Part Two: Companies Worth Owning

The stock market is a public market, not a gaming table. An entrepreneurial investor respects the distinction by using his or her knowledge of business to choose excellent companies for a stock portfolio. This section reviews some of the key concepts that help in the selection process.

7. Who Really Manages a Brand? (Hint: It's Not the Company).

Before you invest, see the company through its customers' eyes. It may take a while for the repercussions of customer service to hit the stock price, but they always get there, for better or worse.

8. What Makes You So Special?

In a fast-paced global economy, competitive advantage is harder to achieve and harder to maintain over time. The best companies can tell you why they are special today, and how they will be special tomorrow.

9. Company Culture Is More Important than Ever.

Make no mistake: Company culture is a key success factor, and grows in importance as companies increasingly depend on highly educated, highly independent workers.

10. Bogie and Bergman Explain Elasticity of Demand.

We're big movie fans, and we're students of economics, so, of course, we noticed lessons on supply, demand, and pricing power in the film *Casablanca.* Understanding the concept of elasticity helps investors make long-term choices.

11. Red Flags and Roaches.

With thousands of stocks to choose from, even an overdiversified investor decides *not* to buy many companies. With a nod to legendary fund manager Peter Lynch, we submit our own guide for avoiding pipe dreams, lies, scoundrels, and scalawags.

12. Inspirational Figures: David Packard.

The cofounder of Hewlett-Packard recognized the importance of company culture—and then *invented* Silicon Valley.

Part Three: The Owner's Manual

High-level math skills and accounting degrees are not required for investing success. Rather, an entrepreneurial investor needs a solid understanding of which numbers are important, and why.

13. Televised Investment Advice: No Worse than Drilling Your Own Teeth.

There's a lot of expert advice available, but who has the most expertise in your individual needs and goals? You do, of course.

14. Lies, Damned Lies, and Financial Statements.

Reading a financial statement requires the right frame of mind and the right set of questions. Most investors ask, "How does this company make money?" The entrepreneurial investor adds, "How does this company make money for *me?*"

15. How to Be an Annual Report Detective.

A lot of important information hides just below the surface of a company's annual report. With the right sleuthing skills, a prospective investor can discover hidden value or raise troubling questions.

16. How Inventory Can Skew the Financials.

Inventory misrepresentation is the most common type of asset valuation fraud, but even with honest, accurate, and consistent accounting methods, inventory levels can hide valuable—or risky—secrets.

17. Great First Impressions: 10 Signs of a Quality Company.

What are the first things we look for when a company catches our attention? Here is a list of 10 easy-to-assess criteria for evaluating what to buy.

18. Inspirational Figures: Bernard Baruch.

Bernard Baruch made—and kept—his fortune by looking beneath the surface of every investment. He was not afraid of the facts, nor was he afraid to act decisively on the facts.

Part Four: What's It Worth—To Me?

To achieve outstanding investment results, one must discover value that others have missed or do not understand. This section covers the search for value from an entrepreneurial point of view.

19. The ABCs of Market Inefficiency.

Entrepreneurial investing is an evolved form of value investing, and value investing is easily understood through the ABCs: Assets, at a Bargain price, with a probable Catalyst.

20. "Wait Till the Moon Is Full."

Patience is the entrepreneurial investor's greatest virtue, particularly when buying stock. Waiting until the price is right makes all the difference in margin of safety and ultimate returns.

21. Today's Price for Tomorrow's Growth: The X Factor.

Predicting the future is tricky enough, but an investor needs tools for understanding how much a company's future is worth today. The X Factor helps us compare competing investment opportunities.

22. *The Long View, and Why Women Are Better Investors.*

Investors face many pressures to trade. Too often, people sell their winners for a quick profit and keep their losers, hoping for a rebound. In the long run, this is a losing strategy.

23. *Intrinsic Value: Putting It All Together.*

The concepts are simple, but the details can be vexing. Here is an overview of our day-to-day process for evaluating what a company is truly worth, regardless of its price.

24. *Inspirational Figures: Howard Hughes.*

Long before he became a caricature of mental illness, Howard Hughes was a national hero, and for good reason. His life teaches the value of focus and passion, and reminds us that money is not everything.

Epilogue: The Fortune Cookie that Ate Wall Street

Common sense is more common than many people believe, but do we have the *confidence* to believe what we see and question what we hear?

PART I

THINK LIKE AN OWNER

THE ART OF THE
ENTREPRENEURIAL INVESTOR

The entrepreneurial investing style is defined by focus, opportunity, and personal involvement.

This section explores five simple ideas behind the entrepreneurial investing style:

- See things for yourself, and trust your own intelligence.
- Cool heads prevail in the stock market.
- Stick to what you know.
- Diversify enough to mitigate risk, but concentrate enough to amplify results.
- Style boxes arbitrarily limit opportunity.

Eyes Believe What They See; Ears Believe Others

Warren Buffett says that one of the most important things he learned from Columbia University professor and value investor Benjamin Graham was this: "You're neither right nor wrong because other people agree with you. You're right because your facts are right and your reasoning is right. That's the only thing that makes you right."[1]

Years earlier, Wall Street legend Bernard Baruch purportedly said that every man is entitled to his own opinion but not to his own facts. However, separating fact from opinion presents challenges in this age of blogs, sound bites, and bumper-sticker philosophizing. Or does it? Maybe we just need to pay attention and look around us.

Pay Attention

In 1992, the *New York Times* reported that President George H. W. Bush was "amazed" by supermarket scanner technology, suggesting that the president was out of touch with the American people, belonging to a caste of aristocrats for whom others did the shopping. Although the story turned out to be apocryphal, evidence suggests there really is an elite group of Americans who haven't done much grocery shopping in recent years—the analysts and institutional investors of Wall Street.

Supermarket chains such as Safeway (SWY), Kroger (KR) and Albertsons have been in trouble for years. The competitive landscape shifted dramatically when retailing giants Wal-Mart (WMT) and Costco (COST) expanded their merchandise lines to include groceries. The trouble had been brewing for a very long time, but Wall Street noticed quite late. We think this situation illustrates the arrogance of overeducation: Investment professionals studied analysts' charts and graphs, but didn't notice the Costco, Trader Joe's, Whole Foods (WFMI), and Wal-Mart grocery bags being unloaded from their neighbors' cars.

Customers seem to know well in advance when a company is in trouble, but Wall Street often notices after the damage is done, then severely punishes the stock.

Backyard Barbecues Predicted Supermarket Sector Decline

Education without experience is knowledge without wisdom. Remember the fortune cookie: "Your eyes believe what they see; your ears believe others." We think anyone could have seen this crisis in the supermarket business coming. Thirty years ago, if you went to a multifamily barbecue, the host bought the meat at a butcher's shop. Ten years ago, the host bought the meat, drinks, and paper goods at the supermarket. For the last five years, the host has bought the meat, drinks, paper goods, lawn furniture, potted plants, outdoor speakers, and barbecue itself at Costco or Wal-Mart.

What goes great with a sport utility vehicle and a giant stainless steel freezer? A huge cargo of dry goods and frozen meats—it's all part of the super-sizing of America. Our huge middle class does not have the cash-flow worries of 30 years ago; they are better able to realize economies of scale by shopping "club" style and buying in bulk. Of course, few top-floor Manhattan restaurants host multifamily barbecues, so quite a few stockbrokers missed this trend until it was too big to miss.

Kodak Fails to Focus on Digital Photography

Long-term investors must distinguish trends from fads. Large companies are, by definition, long-term investors in themselves, but many seem to miss trends that the average person and the competition clearly identify. We cannot say Eastman Kodak (EK) missed the fact that large numbers of people would embrace digital photography, for Kodak was an early entrant into the market and then chief executive officer George Fisher was committed to transforming the company. They simply mishandled it because the entire organization did not buy in. Offering low-priced, feature-poor cameras and very expensive, high-end cameras, Kodak misallocated resources for at least 10 years and remained focused on producing film, utterly missing the mass-market feature set and price points for digital cameras. They also seem to have missed the market for digital media such as compact flash cards, the products that are replacing film.

The company will insist that it was listening to customers. We believe it was listening to marketing focus groups, but it failed to watch customer behavior. In 2001, we noticed a colleague who rhapsodized about the quality of his 35mm Nikon cameras was leaving the 20-pound camera bag at home and taking his tiny digital camera everywhere he went. It's what people do every day that really counts.

Young Adults Herald the Wireless Future

A visit to any college community since 1999 shows the future of telecommunications. School-year renters no longer bother with landline phone service; everyone has cell phones. In these same communities, DirecTV and digital cable systems now deliver television programming and high-speed Internet access. Landline phone companies and dial-up Internet services seemed dumbfounded as their customers fled en masse for the obvious benefits of wireless telephony and high-speed DSL or cable Internet access.

Television Loses Its Reason for Existence

People don't like to acknowledge this, but television news and entertainment are mere subsidiaries of the advertising industry. What will happen as more consumers gain the power to avoid commercials through time-shifting digital recorders like Tivo? The advertising industry is currently reacting with more in-program product placement, which has drawn regulator and consumer advocate attention, but not much revenue.

What is the future of the advertising industry if people have the power to avoid ads? When will the ripples hit content and distribution companies like Viacom (VIA-B), Disney (DIS), and NBC (GE), whose products are paid for by advertising revenue?

Grocers Lose Touch, and Their Identity

Wal-Mart revolutionized retailing through technological mastery of their supply chain, ensuring that the most popular items are always in stock, and always at the lowest prices. With their remarkable distribution and information technology systems in place, conquering grocery retailing must have seemed a simple matter. In fact, in 2001, Wal-Mart surpassed industry leader Kroger with an estimated $65.3 billion in food sales. Somehow, before anyone thought of them as a grocery store, Wal-Mart became the nation's biggest grocer.

Other, smaller competitors position themselves to make traditional supermarket shopping seem like drudgery. People talk about a trip to Trader Joe's as an *event*. A quirky alternative for those who love to experiment with an ever-changing inventory, Trader Joe's offers gourmet fare at discount prices, and does so with humor and personality. Whole Foods positions itself as a morally superior alternative for healthy, environmentally friendly, and socially conscious shopping. It uses its unique identity as its competitive advantage.

Wal-Mart, Costco, and specialty retailers like Whole Foods and Trader Joe's are expanding and taking market share from Albertsons, Safeway, and Kroger. The declining stock prices of these large supermarket chains reflect Wall Street's reaction to the customer exodus.

Frontline Coworkers and Customers

Although Yogi Berra's famous remark that a certain restaurant was "so popular that no one goes there anymore" is an amusing oxymoron, it may have been accurate. Customers know when the wait is too long, and word gets around. As soon as digital photography looked plausible, customers started complaining about the inconvenience of 35mm film—the mystery, waiting, and expense. When decent digital cameras broke the $500 price point, customers bought them.

Was it not clear that as soon as wireless matched the quality of landline telephones, the latter would be redundant? Was it not apparent that everyone using high-speed Internet access at the office would clamor for high-speed access at home?

Did some of the largest companies in America watch their customers, or did they listen to marketing consultants, accountants, stock analysts, and other experts? Did they even listen to their own frontline employees, those firsthand witnesses of customer behavior?

The Smartest Man in the Room?

It's been said that a good writer does not have to be the smartest person in the room, just the most observant. Likewise, a good investor doesn't have to know everything in the world about investing, but ought to know what's going on in the world. We think Wall Street brokers and analysts talk to each other more than they watch consumer behavior. It's interesting to hear how other people invest money, but it's more profitable to watch how consumers spend their money. Pay attention.

In 2003, a strike by supermarket workers put a lot of pressure on supermarket chains and delivered a spike in sales and profits to smaller chains. Figure 1.1 compares supermarket giant Safeway and niche player Arden Group (ARDNA), which owns Gelson's markets. Note that Safeway's and Arden's performance diverged years before the 2003 supermarket strike, but since 2003 Safeway has also underperformed the Standard & Poor's (S&P) 500. Also note that shoppers and investors continue to reward the major supermarkets' competitors long after the strike.

Supermarket chains have been steadily losing ground to niche players who can more profitably serve specific market segments. Costco and Wal-Mart attract price-conscious shoppers, while quirky and upscale markets like Trader Joe's and Gelson's appeal to enthusiasts who are willing to pay for the experience.

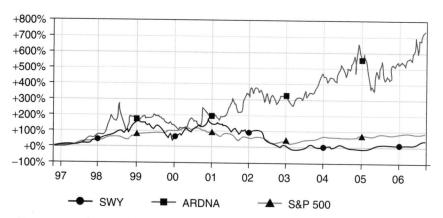

Figure 1.1   Did Shoppers Know before Wall Street?

Data Source: FT Interactive Data via Capital IQ, a division of Standard & Poor's.

Squeezed into the middle, supermarkets that were already competing on razor-thin margins now face serious disruption in their industry. Is it only in hindsight that we could see how the Wal-Mart business model would help them surpass industry leader Kroger so quickly? As someone who likely buys groceries at least once a week, could you have profited from the changes happening around you?

2

Others' Irrationality Is Your Opportunity

At its best, the stock market democratizes capitalism, allowing individuals with limited capital to own shares of companies they wish to support. At its worst, the stock market is a gambling den, where speculators, raconteurs, and outright con men play games with other people's money. With all due respect to the mentally ill, we think the stock market is crazy.

No matter how many rules of thumb and formulae one may apply to the stock market, the market still manages to behave in odd ways. For example, as we write this, oil prices are still quite high, demand is challenging supply, yet many oil company stocks are trading at a fraction of their intrinsic value, even assuming 20 percent lower oil prices. As a result, oil companies have been buying reserves on Wall Street for less than they would spend to discover them in the ground. This is illogical, but not entirely surprising.

Bulls and Bears and Lemmings, Oh My!

When Federal Reserve Chairman Alan Greenspan made his famous 1996 remark about "irrational exuberance" escalating stock values beyond reason, he also spoke of the "unexpected and prolonged contractions" that follow (suggesting they weren't "unexpected" at all).[1]

The stock market's roller-coaster history suggests that irrational exuberance works with a partner: irrational fear. Some say the stock market is like a wonderful cocktail party, except the last person to leave has to clean up. While at the party, everyone has a great time, but everyone also keeps an eye on the door. And when a few people start to leave, a mad rush follows, like lemmings rushing to the sea.

Fear and euphoria cause the market to overreact. For those who keep a cool head, opportunities abound.

When Bad Markets Happen to Good Companies

In the 1997 blockbuster film *Men in Black,* Detective James Edwards says the Men in Black should reveal the truth about extraterrestrials living on Earth:

> "People are smart," he says. "They can handle it."
>
> "A person is smart," replies Agent K. "People are dumb, panicky, dangerous animals and you know it."[2]

Ten years before that film was released, Wall Street proved the point. On October 19, 1987, the Dow Jones Industrial Average dropped over 500 points, losing 22.6 percent of its value. This triggered panic selling in other exchanges worldwide. Yet within two years the market was back at precrash levels, suggesting that actual values were not completely out of line in 1987, but people's emotions were completely out of control.

A logical investor must take irrational market behavior into account when choosing stocks to buy, sell, and hold. Fear and euphoria cannot dominate the actions of someone who really knows the companies and industries in which he or she invests, but other people's fear and euphoria should influence one's choices. Do not blindly follow the herd, but pay close attention to its movements. Opportunity exists in the gap between a company's value and the herd's perception of its value. Of course, it can take a long time for the herd to catch up, but that is how an entrepreneurial investor's patience is rewarded.

Importance of the Long-Term Approach

Long-term thinking is essential because short-term volatility cannot be consistently predicted. But long-term trends allow greater perspective when choosing a stock because large-scale concepts like business cycles and "regression to the mean" improve our ability to evaluate probabilities. In other words, even though no one can predict the future, long-term trends have a higher probability of playing out.

Despite All the Screaming, the Roller Coaster Stays on Track

The late Douglas Adams's hilarious book *The Hitchhiker's Guide to the Galaxy* (Del Rey, 1995) notes that one reason the *Hitchhiker's Guide* is superior to the far more comprehensive *Encyclopedia Galactica* is the fact that, in addition to being less expensive, the *Guide* has etched into its cover two very important words: "Don't Panic." Excellent advice for a galactic sojourner and excellent advice for an intelligent investor.[3]

Because of mob dynamics, the stock market sometimes behaves irrationally. Individuals need not do so. Keep perspective. Prudent investors maintain a "watch list" of quality companies that should be considered when prices drop. When the market dives, we know there are good companies available at bargain prices, and we act, providing the quality of the company has not changed. As long as we do our homework, know what we know and what we don't know, and stick to our long-term philosophy, we do not have to follow the bulls, the bears, or the lemmings.

The price volatility of a company like Noven Pharmaceuticals (NOVN) allows an engaged investor multiple opportunities to buy and sell when it suits him best (see Figure 2.1).

Entrepreneurial investors welcome volatility, and Benjamin Graham's famous "Mr. Market" metaphor explains why. Graham asks

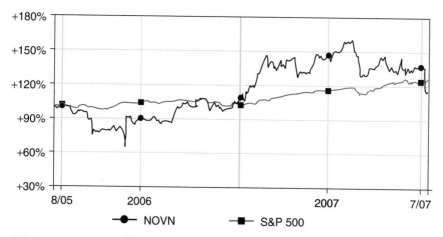

Figure 2.1   How Market Volatility Creates Opportunities for Entrepreneurial Investors

Data Source: FT Interactive Data via Capital IQ, a division of Standard & Poor's.

us to imagine that we are business partners with a slightly impaired gentleman named Mr. Market. Mr. Market is a moody fellow, and every day, depending on how he feels, he knocks on our door and offers to either buy our interest in the company or sell us his.[4]

The prices offered by Mr. Market might be absurdly high or low, or they might be a fair value, based on our understanding of the business. One of the nice things about Mr. Market is that he doesn't mind being ignored; he'll come right back tomorrow with another offer. So we are in the driver's seat. If Mr. Market offers to buy our share of the company for a ridiculously high price, we may take his money. If he offers to sell his share for a ridiculously low price, we can take advantage of the bargain. If, however, he wants to sell for too high a price or buy too low, we may ignore him. After all, he'll be back tomorrow.

The point is this: If we know the actual value of the company, we need only buy or sell when the act benefits us. If we do not understand the value of the company, Mr. Market, foolish though he may be, holds sway over us, and this is trouble. Warren Buffett, citing Graham's parable, reminds us of the old poker axiom, "If you've been in the game 30 minutes and you don't know who the patsy is, you're the patsy." The story of Mr. Market warns us that the stock market exists to serve us, not to guide us.

3

Dirty Harry's Investment Philosophy

In each of Clint Eastwood's *Dirty Harry* films, protagonist Harry Callahan utters a trademark line of dialogue, such as the famous "Go ahead, make my day."[1] Some investors seem to think that the first film's "Do you feel lucky?"[2] is adequate guidance for choosing stocks. We prefer the more mature Inspector Callahan from the 1973 film *Magnum Force.* He wisely noted, "A man's got to know his limitations."[3]

When someone complains that he or she lost money by investing in Enron, we express mild sympathy. Then, we put on our most naïve expression to say, "You know, I've never quite understood what business Enron was in. Could you explain it to me?" We don't want to embarrass these people, but we want them to learn from their mistakes. As far as we can tell, the handful of people who really understood Enron's business actually made a lot of money, although several are facing prison time.

Whether you make your own investment decisions or rely on someone else to make them for you, you must take time and effort to understand what you own. It's your money, and the consequences of its use fall squarely on your shoulders and your wallet.

Can You Explain It to a Child?

Some people view the stock market as an elaborate gaming table. Others see it as a noble democratization of business ownership. Both want the highest possible returns, and they can improve the odds of success by investing in companies that are easy to understand.

Of course, *easy to understand* is a relative term. We know a man who made his fortune investing in obscure areas of nuclear energy and medicine that most of us could not comprehend, but he is a physicist and better able to assess the probability of success.

With thousands of stocks to choose from, a concentrated portfolio of 10 to 15 stocks need not include companies beyond an investor's circle of competence or comfort. To build a portfolio of companies you can live and prosper with, ask this question: "Can I explain this to a six year old?" This may seem extreme, but it will help you understand a company at the level of its most fundamental strengths.

Advantages of Simplicity

With few exceptions, we prefer simple business models that emphasize doing one or two things really well. Consider how easily we can describe some of the consistent top performers of the past 20 years:

Wal-Mart (WMT):	They discount everyday products
Wrigley (WWY):	They make chewing gum
Coca-Cola (KO):	They make soft drinks
ADP (ADP):	They process payroll
American Express (AXP):	They provide credit
Boeing (BA):	They build airplanes

Simplicity alone is not the reason for their success, and all of these companies have their ups and downs. But you have to admit: They are easier to understand than Enron, Cisco Systems (CSCO), or WorldCom.

Over the long term, Wall Street rewards simplicity, because a company attracts investors by demonstrating that it knows how to profit, generate cash flow, and maintain competitive advantage. The market sometimes loses sight of this; in the 1990s people touting the "new economy" said some very cruel things about Warren Buffett because he "just didn't get it." Buffett's eventual vindication was a triumph for entrepreneurial investors everywhere.

When considering the purchase of stock, remember that if you can clearly understand the business, so can the coworkers, customers, creditors, and other investors, all of whom influence the stock price. Plus, you may better understand how social, political, and financial events and trends affect your company.

What If You Were CEO?

Note that in the preceding sentence we said "your company," because that is how an entrepreneurial investor views the ownership of stock. Financial columnist David Forrest regularly asks his readers whether, if they had the money, they would buy the whole company in which they wish to invest. It's a fair question. When you buy stock, you are buying a fractional part of the whole company; the difference is merely a matter of scale.

Whether you're spending a little or a lot, you are buying the company's character. Some people don't want to own companies involved in animal research, factory farming, tobacco, or weaponry, but are stunned to discover divisions of their own holdings are involved in such businesses. Others may be bothered not by the type of work being done, but by the culture or ethics of the organization.

But more to our original point: Would you be willing to own a company you do not understand at all? What if you were also CEO? How would you manage a business with dozens of subsidiaries or an unclear business model? If you would not be willing to buy the entire business, why would you own a portion of it?

How can you learn about companies that interest you but are not quite as simple as Coca-Cola? The company's branding and marketing efforts can help or hinder the process of understanding; we tend to discount self-promotion in our analysis. While there is no substitute for face-to-face interviews with the company's customers and coworkers ("your eyes believe what they see; your ears believe others"), this is impractical for most people.

Still, it is relatively easy to access Securities and Exchange Commission (SEC) filings, including a company's annual report, quarterly reports, proxy statements, and insider holdings data. No matter what else you read about a company, review the 10-K and proxy statement filed with the SEC. This should provide a clear picture of the company and its leaders. Most of all, use your eyes. Learn what you can about the company and its products from customers and coworkers. Whenever possible, be a customer!

It also helps to choose companies that operate within your own field of expertise. If you are a geologist, you have an edge when evaluating oil and natural gas exploration companies. If you are a house painter, you know whose paints and rollers are good quality.

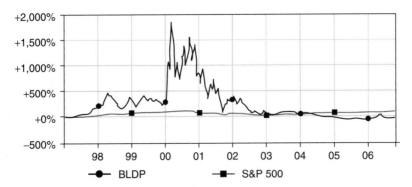

Figure 3.1   Too Little Knowledge Is a Dangerous Thing

Data Source: FT Interactive Data via Capital IQ, a division of Standard & Poor's.

Limitations Provide Boundaries for Focus

As investors, we feel that the only thing more important than knowing what we know is knowing what we don't know. We understand chewing gum better than we understand proton exchange membrane fuel cells. We know a lot more about finance and real estate than we do about gene therapy. We focus on what we know in an attempt to meet our long-term capital appreciation objectives, staying within our "circle of competence," as Warren Buffett calls it. Like Inspector Harry Callahan, we know our limitations, but we do not let them limit our success.

Back in early 2000, an associate of ours thought he'd found a golden opportunity to invest in Ballard Power (BLDP), a company that develops fuel cell technology (see Figure 3.1). His general reasoning was sound: The price was dragged from its high by the bursting of the tech bubble, and it seemed obvious that alternative fuel sources would be needed in the future. Plus, this fellow knew an engineer at Ballard who frequently praised the company's innovations.

Of course, good reasoning based on the wrong set of facts gets people in trouble. Ballard may in fact be a fantastic company, but our friend knew nothing about fuel cell technology, nothing about the time frame for profitability of this or any other fuel cell company, and . . . well, we don't have space to list everything he didn't understand.

He stepped far outside his circle of competence; bought the stock at approximately $30 per share; and later, frustrated, sold it at approximately $8 per share. Stick to what you understand.

4

Adversity in Diversity: Portfolio Concentration

The most critical—and controversial—attribute of our investing style is our commitment to a concentrated portfolio. At any given time, we hold as few as 10 stocks, and rarely more than 15. The very thought of this causes amateur investors to swoon. Everyone seems to believe that broad diversification improves safety, but we strongly disagree. Few seem to understand that overdiversification also reduces returns. Investors diversify their holdings to reduce the risk that a single company's poor performance might irreparably damage their net worth. But wide diversification doesn't eliminate risk; rather, it presents a different kind of risk.

How much diversification is necessary to manage risk, and at what point does diversification reduce portfolio performance? To answer this question, let us first understand systematic and unsystematic risk. Systematic risk, also known as market risk, refers to the gyrations of the stock market as a whole; this is considered beyond the control of individuals. For example, a highly diversified index fund that emulates the Standard & Poor's (S&P) 500 will rise and fall with the market itself. Current events and other macroeconomic stimuli that affect the stock market create risk that affects the entire system, hence the expression *systematic risk.*

Unsystematic risk, also known as specific risk, refers to the risk attached to individual companies. This is what investors attempt to manage through diversification. If you invest 100 percent of your net worth in First Little Pig, Inc., and it declares bankruptcy after a light wind destroys its factory (built of straw), you've lost your fortune. If you had one third of your assets in each of Second Little Pig, Inc., and Third Little Pig, Inc., your unsystematic risk is spread over three companies, two of which use better building materials in their factories. If you own hundreds of little pig companies (small-cap); hundreds of big bad wolves (large-cap), and hundreds of straw, stick, and brick companies (construction and technology), your exposure to unsystematic risk diminishes almost entirely, but so do your chances of outperforming the market, because your portfolio now closely resembles the entire market.

Relying on diversification alone to manage risk is a lazy investor's way to protect assets from unsystematic risk. This is what most mutual funds do, but fund performance tends to mirror the general market. After fees, mutual funds underperform over the long term, with few exceptions.

Instead of seeking safety in numbers, entrepreneurial investors seek safety in knowledge; a concentrated portfolio allows intimate knowledge of the holdings.

It surprises most people to learn that unsystematic risk can be meaningfully reduced by owning as few as 15 stocks. Statistically, one achieves only minimal reduction in risk when diversifying beyond 20 stocks.

But concentration by itself is not a virtue; judicious stock selection makes concentration work, as we demonstrate in Part Two of this book: Companies Worth Owning.

Are Concentrated Portfolios Worth the Effort?

Minimal diversification coupled with careful selection of individual stocks can provide adequate risk reduction, but why go to all this trouble if wide diversification achieves the same thing? While preserving capital is a high priority, it is not our only objective. Concentrated portfolios tend to outperform widely diversified portfolios. In his book *The Warren Buffett Portfolio* (John Wiley & Sons, Inc., 1999), Robert Hagstrom compared the returns of large portfolios (250 stocks) against portfolios of 15 stocks. Only 2 percent of the large portfolios beat the market, but over 25 percent of the small portfolios performed better than the overall market.

Keep in mind, however, that concentrated portfolios were also more likely to underperform the market; thus, we see the importance of stock selection. Concentrated portfolios allow individual stocks to significantly impact performance, albeit positive or negative. Wide diversification limits the amount one can invest in a specific company, but proponents of concentration tend to invest large amounts in individual companies when research indicates the odds are in their favor. This can increase risk, but also maximizes gains.

Along with unsystematic risk comes the concept of unsystematic gains, or "alpha," as it's known in the investment industry. This refers to the gains attributed to an investor's skill, as opposed to systematic gains achieved via general market forces ("beta"). A concentrated portfolio allows us to select more judiciously, to thoroughly understand the companies, to respond quickly and powerfully to opportunities, and to take advantage of tax efficiencies when buying and selling.

We're in good company with our preference for concentrated portfolios: master investor Warren Buffett (Berkshire Hathaway [BRKA]) also believes in holding a small number of excellent companies, procured at discount prices. When the subject of concentration comes up, we usually quote Buffett, who offers the following comment:

> I cannot understand why an investor elects to put money into a business that is his 20th favorite rather than simply adding that money to his top choices—the businesses he understands best and present the least risk, along with the greatest profit potential.[1]

Why indeed.

Careful selection makes a concentrated portfolio work. First of all, an entrepreneurial investor seeking to limit potential losses requires a margin of safety, such as tangible assets or a strong competitive advantage. Reducing the likelihood of losses also helps to magnify the effect of strong performers within the portfolio.

In any given year or two, a concentrated portfolio can generate strong results from the performance of only one or two stocks, because care is taken to bet big when the odds are in the investor's favor. In the example above, Wrigley's (WWY) unfortunate underperformance has been comparatively small, while ATP Oil & Gas (ATPG) has performed impressively (see Figure 4.1). If each of these stocks represented 1 percent of your portfolio, the impact would have been minimal. But in a 15-stock portfolio, each might represent 5 to

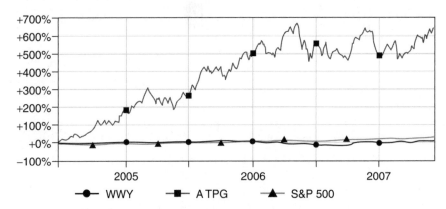

Figure 4.1   Letting One Stock Make a Difference

Data Source: FT Interactive Data via Capital IQ, a division of Standard & Poor's.

15 percent of the total, in which case the Wrigley loss is still trivial, but the ATP gain is significant where it counts most: in dollars.

Berkshire Hathaway, managed by Warren Buffett and Charlie Munger, exemplifies the advantages of a concentrated portfolio. As of March 31, 2007, Berkshire Hathaway reported holding public equities valued at over $57 billion. Berkshire had 42 holdings, of which the top 10 represented 81.5 percent of the portfolio's market value. The top 5 positions represented 61.6 percent of the portfolio's total market value. As Buffett and Munger frequently point out and demonstrate, a fortune can be made with very few stock purchases.

Munger has also provided the ultimate metaphor for overdiversification: "When you mix raisins with turds, you've still got turds."[2] In other words, choose quality over quantity.

CHAPTER 5

Just Buy the Best (Which Does Not Include Most Mutual Funds)

Market capitalization (stock price times shares outstanding) may help us evaluate whether an individual company is over- or undervalued, compared to peers. But some people view large-cap (typically over $10 billion in value), small-cap (typically under $1.5 billion), and mid-cap companies as segments of their own, and many fund managers limit themselves to large- or small-cap stocks exclusively. They group stocks into a matrix based on size and style (value, growth, or mixed). To us, these style boxes seem more like a marketing gimmick than an investment philosophy.

Convenient Carrying Handles

When you're selling ideas and services, consumers need "convenient carrying handles" so they can easily "pick up" what you offer. Thus, mutual fund and portfolio managers package their services as products with easy-to-remember descriptions: "a large-cap value fund" or a "small-cap growth portfolio."

The marketing of these products benefits from tenets of conventional wisdom about the respective attributes of large- and small-cap stocks:

- Large-cap and small-cap segments alternate periods of outperforming the market.
- During an economic recovery, small-caps do better because they are nimble.

- Post recovery, large-caps perform better because of earnings scale and dividends.
- By virtue of their size, large-cap stocks are more secure.
- One should balance asset allocation based on cap size.

Although these statements are sometimes true and can certainly help one decide between two funds designed around these beliefs, they are also dramatic oversimplifications that do not help one choose the most effective investment for one's individual needs. Besides, entrepreneurs excel at proving the conventional wisdom wrong.

Conventional Wisdom Equals Conventional Results

Packaged investment products more or less define conventional wisdom through market cap and valuation categories. Still, these semantic exercises spring from reasonably credible trends: in general, small companies have more room to grow than giant companies, and, in general, large companies are less volatile than small companies. Of course, in general, actively managed mutual funds underperform when compared to the Standard & Poor's (S&P) 500. That's why we eschew the general in favor of the specific.

We would call adherence to the conventional wisdom a lazy man's approach to investing, except that there is no reason even a lazy man should arbitrarily limit his opportunities to companies of a certain size or valuation category. A smart lazy man would simply invest in low-fee market index funds and benefit from the long-term performance of the market as a whole. But for anyone seeking superior results from their investments, conventional wisdom does not suffice.

A Simple Failure of Logic

The lure of "large-cap" and "small-cap" as convenient carrying handles is understandable but misguided. Why would anyone insist on buying large-cap stocks if there were better opportunities in small- or mid-cap stocks, or vice versa? In a marketplace where opportunities may appear anywhere and at any time, inflexibility is a liability.

Moreover, the conventional wisdom may not be very wise. For example, the security ascribed to large-caps may be little more than a self-fulfilling prophecy: Large fund and pension managers believe they must own large-cap stocks for security, so they keep buying them, increasing the demand for shares and keeping the price high, regardless of the company's quality or intrinsic value. Seeking security, they build a house of cards. Expect any large-cap fund to own General Electric, just as they owned Enron, WorldCom, JDS Uniphase (JDSU), and so on.

More specialized funds also tend to exert a circular influence. If, for example, the fund requires a specific allocation of resources to technology stocks, a finite number of companies fit that definition. The money must be invested within a narrow selection of companies, regardless of other factors. This artificially inflates prices and, in extreme cases, could cause a market bubble. We may be seeing this today in "emerging markets."

What Do You Invest For?

Market capitalization isn't the whole story of any company, but it provides an interesting means of comparison. For General Electric's market cap of $383 billion (June 2007), one could buy Walt Disney (DIS), Automatic Data Processing, Wrigley, Costco, Hershey, Tiffany (TIF), Apple Computer, Molson Coors, Safeway, Xerox, and a small country or two.

Each of these companies has its own problems developing new products, finding new markets, and expanding market share. In other words, growth is difficult for these icons of capitalism; imagine how hard it is for GE.

However, if you buy a small-cap fund, you will miss the advantages of well-run, dividend-producing giants like Johnson & Johnson (JNJ). If you invest in both large-cap and small-cap funds, you may earn average market returns, but with higher fees than a simple index fund. What's the point?

Why Is Poor Performance So Popular?

A brilliant idea at their inception, mutual funds allow "the little guy" to buy shares of an already-diversified portfolio. The benefits of wide diversification are particularly attractive to those who require some sense of security, despite the inherent risks of investing. Are mutual funds still a brilliant idea, or have they sacrificed performance for perceived security?

While there are thousands of funds with ostensibly unique management philosophies, the consumer's growing need for security has driven mutual funds to overdiversify; the more stocks they own, the more average their results. Simple index funds (a type of mutual fund designed to approximate market measurement indices, such as the Dow Jones Industrial Average or the S&P 500) routinely outperform the vast majority of actively managed stock mutual funds.

This is because index funds generally achieve similar capital appreciation (due to the high number of stocks and correlation to the market), but charge much lower fees than most actively managed funds. Mutual funds usually include sales charges and high expense ratios, including management fees, load fees, administrative costs, distribution fees, and various operating expenses.

Thus, mutual funds exhibit some of the worst habits of untrained individual investors, including excessive trading (average turnover of 80 to 112 percent), crystal ball attempts at market timing, and indifference to tax efficiencies. But the fees generated by mutual funds pay for a lot of marketing, and the segment keeps growing. Ironically, many providers of mutual funds are better investments than their funds, thanks to fee income from a consumer and 401(k) market hungry for "safe" investments. Sadly, most mutual fund investors are not even aware of the vast web of fees they are paying, even though these fees must be disclosed. Like most mandated communications, the disclosures are often incomprehensible to the layman.

Funds Cannot Serve Individuals

As an investment "pool" for thousands or hundreds of thousands of investors, mutual funds are "packaged goods." An individual can buy or sell shares of the fund, but cannot control any other aspect, such as the timing of individual stock sales or purchases within the fund. In fact, mutual fund investors do not actually own the stocks in the fund, only an interest in the fund itself. Because individuals cannot control the sales within a mutual fund, they cannot manage the tax consequences.

Many companies offer a wide range of mutual funds, but typically advertise only the ones with the best performance. Of course, past performance is no guarantee of future results. The really great fund managers sometimes end up managing so much money that their choices become constrained. As you can imagine, it's a lot more challenging to invest $15 billion than $500 million. For one thing, they have to buy a lot more stocks and/or much larger companies;

this drives performance closer to the market average. But if they buy too much of any one company, they risk a loss of liquidity because there may not be a market for their shares, or the sale of their shares may be too disruptive to the share price. Often, the best managers move on to more lucrative "hedge funds," or simply devote more time to managing their own accumulated wealth, acquired largely through client fees.

A Las Vegas tourism billboard on the I-15 freeway in California proclaimed "Seven Deadly Sins; One Convenient Location." This sums up our feelings about most mutual funds, which are a repository for bad investing habits. Many people do not have the time and research resources to manage their investments, and this is one reason mutual funds have been so popular, despite their mediocre performance.

Just Buy the Best

Small, custom portfolios of stocks, selected for individual quality and value, have the ability to outperform funds of any kind, and careful investors like Warren Buffett and Marty Whitman have been proving this for many years. The key to a successful concentrated portfolio is to limit the number of stocks held, not the number of stocks considered. Entrepreneurs understand the importance of core competencies and the importance of leveraging those core competencies in as many ways as possible. In a concentrated stock portfolio, one needs to find the best values within one's circle of competence, regardless of size or shape. Our circle of competence is limiting enough; we don't need additional restrictions.

We don't care if a stock is large-cap, small-cap, or beanie-cap; we use a broad range of criteria for judging its potential risks and rewards. Limiting ourselves to a certain size of company makes no sense to us. Rather, we seek to understand the company's value, competitive advantage, culture, management, industry, vision, and so on. We urge investors not to tie their own hands by getting caught up in "convenient handles" like large-cap value and small-cap growth. Reducing our investment philosophy to its simplest terms, we advocate this: "Just buy the best."

Johnson & Johnson (JNJ) is a component of the Dow Jones Industrial Average (DJIA), but as you can see, JNJ handily outperforms the group as a whole (see Figure 5.1). This reinforces our

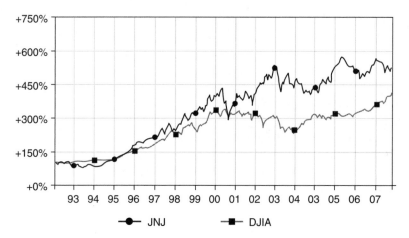

Figure 5.1 One Dow Stock vs. a DJIA Index Fund

Data Source: FT Interactive Data via Capital IQ, a division of Standard & Poor's.

desire to seek out and invest in the best individual companies rather than broad categories.

Our disdain for mutual funds moderates slightly for index funds because of their lower fees, but as you can see, JNJ has delivered considerably better returns than the DJIA and, by extension, index funds approximating the DJIA. Moreover, the safety investors seek through the built-in diversification of index funds is, to some extent, achieved through the scope of JNJ's multiple business units in pharmaceuticals, medical equipment, consumer goods, and the like.

When we say "just buy the best," we're recommending the knockout combination of a concentrated portfolio, a go-anywhere style, and a research methodology that prioritizes intrinsic value, margin of safety, and upside potential. This captures the key attributes of the entrepreneurial investing style: focus, opportunism, and personal involvement.

CHAPTER 6

Inspirational Figures: Benjamin Graham

"If I have seen further, it is by standing on the shoulders of giants," said Sir Isaac Newton, in praise of his predecessors. Today's most successful investors, including Warren Buffett, pay similar homage to a man known as the father of value investing: Benjamin Graham.

Graham was the first to bring a grounded, rational sensibility to Wall Street, distinguishing speculation from investing. During his long career as an investor and educator, Graham sought to distill his findings into a clear and accessible method that would help anyone make better investment decisions. To the benefit of all who study his work, he achieved that goal. Unfortunately, and despite nearly constant praise from his famous followers, few people pay heed to Graham's excellent advice. Fortunately, it is still very good advice.

A Fine Mind, Working Hard

Born in England in 1894, Graham immigrated with his family to the United States before his second birthday. After the death of his father when Graham was just nine years old, the family's importing business fell on hard times, making Benjamin's childhood one of privation and worry. Young Benjamin poured his energy and ambition into his schooling, and made his way to Columbia University, where he earned a bachelor's degree.

An excellent student at Columbia, Graham was offered teaching positions in the mathematics, philosophy, and English departments.

Perhaps owing to the financial insecurity of his youth, Graham instead chose a career on Wall Street, starting out in 1914 as a "chalker" for the firm of Newburger, Henderson, and Loeb. Still an excellent student, by 1919 the 25-year-old was a partner at the firm and exceedingly prosperous.

Roaring Twenties

In 1926, Benjamin Graham entered into two relationships that would come to define his adult life. With Jerome Newman, he formed an investment partnership. He also began teaching a finance course at Columbia University. Students appreciated the fact that their professor spoke from experience about investing. But, as we've often heard, experience is a harsh teacher, because the lesson comes after the test, as it did in 1929.

The stock market crash that began in October 1929 almost wiped out Graham and Newman's company, and did wipe out Graham's personal fortune. But it also opened his eyes to a new way of thinking about investing. Graham's rapid rise and more rapid fall in the 1920s set the stage for a classic American success story, in which a man of sturdy character and great ability achieves stunning victories after surviving horrific defeat.

Great Investor, Great Educator

When Benjamin Graham bent his considerable intellectual abilities to divining a rational alternative to the prevailing speculative nature of stock market investing, he could have kept his methods to himself and profited handsomely. In fact, he did profit handsomely; between the crash of 1929 and his retirement in 1956, Graham's partnership with Newman generated annualized returns of about 17 percent. But Graham was a teacher, in the highest sense of the word, and wanted to make his discoveries available to everybody.

In 1934, Graham and coauthor David Dodd published *Security Analysis*, which to this day has never been out of print and has been a standard textbook for students of finance. The book provides, for the first time in history, a rational and systematic approach for measuring the value of a public company, clearly distinguishing what is knowable from what is mere assumption. The current review on Amazon.com calls *Security Analysis* "hands-down the most influential investment book in history."

While *Security Analysis* became part of the required canon for investment professionals, the book intimidated laymen. Moreover, Graham, like any truth seeker, constantly reviewed and refined his beliefs, hoping to establish clear and simple explanations of complex relationships. He succeeded in 1949, publishing *The Intelligent Investor* (HarperBusiness Essentials, 2005), which Warren Buffett has called "the best book on investing ever written."

Benjamin Graham continually updated his books, and published many articles in periodicals. Three of Graham's ideas make up the core of the "value investing" philosophy and represent, in our opinion, the most important considerations for novice investors (and rational professionals).

Buy Companies, Not Pieces of Paper

One of the strongest points Graham repeated throughout his career emphasized the importance of distinguishing investing from speculation, and choosing only to engage in the former. "Investing is most intelligent when it is most businesslike," wrote Graham. He insisted that stock not be viewed as a piece of paper bought and sold based on price, but as a share of ownership in a real company. Thus, as in our own entrepreneurial investing style, Graham focused on the company, not the stock; the value, not the price.

Value investors exercise more patience than speculative investors, heeding Graham's observation that "In the short run, the market is a voting machine, but in the long run it is a weighing machine." In other words, day-to-day prices fluctuate according to opinion, but in the long term, a company will be valued according to facts.

The facts add up to "intrinsic value," which lies at the heart of value investing. Value investors are bargain hunters, seeking companies that trade at a discount to their intrinsic value, buying when the market misunderstands the value, and profiting when the market eventually recognizes it.

Profiting from Mr. Market's Folly

Value based on fact, rather than opinion, brings us to Graham's most beloved metaphor, the parable of Mr. Market. To illustrate the proper attitude toward the stock market, Graham asks us to imagine that we are business partners with a slightly unhinged gentleman named Mr. Market. Mr. Market is a moody fellow, and every day, depending on how he feels, he offers to either buy our interest in the company or sell us his.

As we explained in Chapter 2, the prices offered by Mr. Market might be absurdly high or low, or they might be a fair value, based on our understanding of the business. One of the nice things about Mr. Market is that he doesn't mind being ignored; he'll come right back tomorrow with another offer. So we are in the driver's seat. If Mr. Market offers to buy our share of the company for a ridiculously high price, we may take his money. If he offers to sell his share for a ridiculously low price, we can take advantage of the bargain. If, on the other hand, he wants to sell for too high a price, or buy too low, we may ignore him. After all, he'll be back tomorrow.

The point is this: If we know the actual value of the company, we need only buy or sell when the act benefits us. If we do not understand the value of the company, Mr. Market, foolish though he may be, holds sway over us, and this is trouble. Warren Buffett, citing Graham's parable, reminds us of the old poker axiom, "If you've been in the game 30 minutes and you don't know who the patsy is, you're the patsy." The story of Mr. Market is meant to remind us that the stock market exists to serve us, not to guide us. Our knowledge of business allows us to profit from others' folly, rather than participate in it. Value investors make volatility their friend.

Margin of Safety

In our opinion, "margin of safety" is the most important concept advanced by Benjamin Graham, and empowers Warren Buffett's first rule of investing: "Never lose money." After all, if making money is the goal of investing, losing money is, to say the least, counterproductive. Thus, intelligent investors seek an adequate margin of safety through very conservative valuation of a company's assets.

In effect, the ultimate margin of safety would exist when a company's market capitalization added up to less than the value of its net assets. In other words, if you could buy the company for $1 million, but it held $1.2 million in cash and real estate and carried no debt, it would be pretty hard to lose money. Of course, a margin of safety could also include secure cash-flow sources, such as long-term contracts.

Margin of safety answers the investor's question, "What is the worst that could happen?" By basing margin of safety on knowable values, such as tangible assets, rather than on speculative concepts, such as "goodwill," one can build a very secure portfolio. Moreover, because one seeks bargain opportunities to "buy a dollar for 50 cents," a portfolio with strong margin-of-safety companies also offers strong opportunity for asset appreciation.

On the Shoulders of Giants

Benjamin Graham died in 1976, shortly after completing the fourth revision of *The Intelligent Investor.* In 1994, at a tribute celebrating the 100th anniversary of his birth, Graham's most famous student, Warren Buffett, spoke about the ideas mentioned earlier: investment as ownership of a company, Mr. Market, and margin of safety.

> I think those three ideas 100 years from now will still be regarded as the three cornerstones, essentially, of sound investment. And that's what Ben was all about. He wasn't about brilliant investing. He wasn't about fads or fashion. He was about sound investing. And what's nice is that sound investing can make you very wealthy if you're not in too big a hurry. And it never makes you poor, which is even better.

Benjamin Graham, despite a financially insecure childhood and severe reversals of fortune as a young man, applied his curiosity, keen observation skills, and analytical mind to the discovery of a rational approach to investing. That he succeeded is impressive. That he chose to share his findings for the benefit of all is more impressive. Columbia University still offers Graham's class on value investing, now taught by Bruce Greenwald, whose *Value Investing: From Graham to Buffett and Beyond* (John Wiley & Sons, 2001) is a worthy companion to *The Intelligent Investor.*

Many investing methodologies derive from Graham's approach, including our own entrepreneurial style. Obsessed as we are with intrinsic value, margin of safety, and resistance to the disadvantageous entreaties of Mr. Market, we owe much of our success, as do many of our peers, to the teachings of Benjamin Graham.

PART
II

COMPANIES WORTH OWNING

Entrepreneurial investors focus on individual companies and their leadership, drawing on business experience and common sense to identify those worthy of investment. We view the stock market as a business opportunity. The market provides a chance to share the risks and rewards of ownership without the physical effort of running the business. This part details some of the ideas we use to evaluate which companies we would like to own:

- Before you invest, see through the customers' eyes.
- Competitive advantage is the one true source of long-term profitability.
- Company culture is a key success factor, and a key failure factor!
- Understand elasticity of demand for better long-term investing.
- Common warning signs make it easy to say "no, thanks."

CHAPTER 7

Who Really Manages the Brand?
(Hint: It's Not the Company)

In the documentary *The Thin Blue Line*, attorney Melvin Carson Bruder says, "Prosecutors in Dallas have said for years—any prosecutor can convict a guilty man. It takes a great prosecutor to convict an innocent man."[1] Too many business executives seem to believe that anyone can sell a product with real value, but it takes a marketing genius to sell products that nobody needs or really wants. Advertising spending generally varies inversely to a product's actual value to consumers, so junk food, fashion, tobacco, alcohol, and soft drinks seem to dominate the airwaves, magazines, and billboards. Lacking competitive advantage, they seek a psychological advantage. For valueless offerings, branding is the great marketing challenge. For companies that provide superior value to customers, clear communication is the great marketing challenge.

After deregulation and the breakup of AT&T's monopoly, a staggering percentage of the company's advertising was spent trying to win back lost customers. With all this spending, and all the advertising spending that accompanied the technology/Internet boom of the 1990s, the simple truth about brands was missed completely. You can fool some of the people all of the time, and all of the people some of the time, but brands are built through customer experience, not fancy marketing. And great brands are destroyed by customer experience, not competition.

This is why an investor must take pains to see a company through its customers' eyes and to be a customer whenever possible.

Accountability: Who Pays the Piper?

"Branding" has become a touchstone for marketing executives who seek to avoid accountability for business concepts like "sales" and "profits." Certainly, we saw the concept of branding abused during the technology bubble of the 1990s. Meaningless, expensive television ads tried to create awareness of brand names without offering any value proposition or clear message of any kind. Note that the collapse of the technology bubble began shortly after the 2000 Super Bowl, rife as it was with incoherent and offensively wasteful advertising. Of course, up to that time, if the objective was to trick people into buying stock, we suppose the ads could be considered very effective. The morally bankrupt advertising industry does not care; it gets paid either way.

We believe that a strong brand is important. A company's brand should instantly telegraph everything good and valuable about the organization. A great reputation helps a company overcome short-term difficulties, particularly if the brand is positively associated with deeply held values, such as Johnson & Johnson during the Tylenol poisonings. (In 1982, seven people in Chicago died after taking Tylenol capsules that had been laced with cyanide. Even though the tampering was localized, Johnson & Johnson put its customers first and immediately recalled *every* bottle of Tylenol in the country—approximately 31 million bottles, with a retail value of more than $100 million. Its handling of the crisis is a legendary case study on the importance of values over valuables.)

But a well-known brand is a double-edged sword, because it also carries with it every negative association with the company. Once tainted, a brand must fight long and hard to overcome devaluing connotations. One can hardly think of Ford without thinking of exploding Pintos, rolling SUVs, layoffs, and financial disaster. And one can hardly see the AT&T logo without thinking of its horrid, relentless telemarketers.

We prefer to invest in companies with instantly clear value propositions because providing real value to customers creates sustainable competitive advantage. To consistently deliver high value to customers, a company must value its customers above all else.

Hubris at the Mountaintop

Brands like Kodak, Sears, Xerox, and AT&T, all seemingly eternal icons of our youth, now carry unwanted baggage with their famous names. These companies all made it to the absolute top of their respective industries; in fact, they invented their industries! They scaled the mountain, and from the mountaintop they could see everything—everything except the mountain.

These companies, for a critical time at least, lost the capacity for honest self-appraisal. Their brands became so powerful, they seemed to believe they could do no wrong. So Sears cut back on customer service, Kodak started bullying its customers, Xerox gave away innovations and sat complacently while competitors overtook its products, and AT&T . . . well, AT&T started making prank phone calls.

These companies lost respect for their customers. They not only failed to pay the piper, they forgot who the piper was. They did not just lose customers—they created enemies.

A Sad State of Affairs

We hate to see great companies lose their way. AT&T must have believed its telemarketing programs were working because it persisted, despite considerable consumer outrage. Competitors even ridiculed AT&T's tactics in national television campaigns.

Brands are formed through customer experience. Conventional wisdom holds that a satisfied customer might tell two or three people, but an unhappy customer tells at least nine. Clever advertising can fool all of the people some of the time, but word of mouth remains the most trustworthy and powerful of all forms of marketing.

For West Coast Asset Management, this story is a sober reminder that customer loyalty is the bedrock on which future earnings are built. And while the day-to-day performance of the stock market may be driven by emotional and psychological factors, earnings drive its long-term performance.

Poor customer service, arrogant management, and misplaced values will eventually destroy even the most powerful brands. Customers and investors are alike; they vote with their dollars. We look for companies that demonstrate a genuine obsession with customer service. These are brands that can create and maintain competitive advantage.

At one time, Eastman Kodak (EK) and Xerox (XRX) were unassailable icons of American industry and marketing (see Figure 7.1).

Today, both companies struggle. Many digital photographers shoot, store, process, print, and display their images without ever

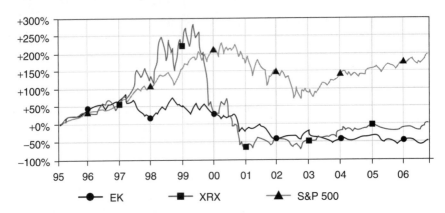

Figure 7.1 Brand Mismanagement

Data Source: FT Interactive Data, via Capital IQ, a division of Standard & Poor's.

touching the Kodak brand. Meanwhile, office workers make "Xerox" copies on a wide variety of other companies' machines.

At this point in history, it's hard to tell whether these companies can offer anything of value aside from their names, which are losing value quickly. Where is Kodak's once legendary connection to Everyman's everyday memories? Where is Xerox's legendary engineering and service?

Kodak and Xerox misjudged their competition and their own core competencies, and the brands lost their meaning. Customers abandoned them, and Wall Street followed.

What Makes You So Special?

The bitterly contested presidential election of 2000 is a case study in bad marketing. When you focus obsessively on your competition, the best you can hope to create is parity. Only by focusing on your customers can you innovate and create competitive advantage. Al Gore and George W. Bush talked only about each other, and the country split down the middle. Failure to establish a unique, compelling position may be considered good election-year politics, but we don't think so, and we think it is bad marketing.

As investment researchers, we are keenly interested in the attributes that make one company more profitable than its competitors over time. We want to invest in companies that distinguish themselves. We want to invest in companies with unique, sustainable competitive advantage.

Attributes of Superior Performers

Competitive advantage exists in any organization that consistently profits more than similar companies. Many characteristics might create such an advantage, but they generally fall into one of two categories: market differentiation and cost structure.

Differentiation refers to any number of attributes that might separate one company from another, such as product quality, customer service, intellectual property, regulatory benefits, and annuity revenue streams. *Cost structures* include innovations, efficiencies, contracts, distribution positions, and shrewd purchasing decisions that produce long-term cost savings unavailable to competitors.

Yet, in either category, a true competitive advantage must be hard to copy, sustainable over time, a barrier to entry, a generator of real value, and adaptable to changing conditions. Entrepreneurs know that competitive advantage is impossible to sustain forever, that strategic planning is really the process of imagining new competitive advantages for the future.

Real-World Examples

Peter Lynch illustrated competitive advantage through the example of owning the only gravel pit in a growing community. The owner can maintain high margins because there is plenty of demand, but competition must endure the expense of shipping a very heavy product from far away.

Johnson & Johnson, Wrigley, and Hallmark present good examples of long-term competitive advantage. JNJ focuses on the constant reinforcement of trust, and has done so from its earliest days. Whether in pharmaceuticals, medical devices, or consumer products, brand equity works as well for JNJ as it does for anyone, and it protects its brand at all costs.

Wrigley leverages the large market for its products by offering a very wide variety and thereby dominating the limited shelf space available for impulse purchases.

Like Wrigley, Hallmark's size, scope, and market share create competitive advantage. Well over half of all greeting cards sold are Hallmark cards. As a result, much of Hallmark's advertising does not emphasize the brand; instead, it conveys the emotional benefits of communicating with cards. Encourage the use of cards, and odds are good that people will buy Hallmark.

Turning Small Sales into Big Business

Recurring revenues are a great source of competitive advantage. Everyone knows the concept of giving away shaving razors and selling the blades, or low-cost ink-jet printers that use expensive ink cartridges. These are good sources of recurring revenue, but long-term contracts are even better. For example, wireless phone and Internet service providers create competitive advantage to the extent that their contracts make it difficult for customers to switch providers.

Strategic alliances also bolster competitive advantage. DataProse, Inc., a private company that prints and mails water bills, partnered with software developers who sell accounting programs to munici-palities. Now they possess expertise and endorsements unavailable to their competitors. Creative managers seek out these kinds of "tiebreakers" so they always have an edge.

Long-term commitments also create competitive advantage. Consider Four Seasons Hotels, which contracts to manage existing properties for other owners. Does the company negotiate for a 5- or 10-year contract? No, its average management contract term is over 50 years! Thus, the company can focus on managing the property, not negotiating the next contract. And competitors? They have to wait a while.

Abuse It and Lose It?

One of the strongest possible competitive advantages is patentable innovation. Many innovations can be copied, but strong patents, such as those in the pharmaceutical industry, can protect a compa-ny's profits for many years.

Some competitive advantages are so strong they invite attack. Microsoft's (MSFT) amazing history might lead some to say that sheer audacity is their primary competitive advantage, but there is no debate that their ubiquity now constitutes a powerful edge in the marketplace—too powerful, according to the Department of Justice and many state attorneys general.

Likewise, Anheuser Busch (BUD), which holds a dramatic advan-tage in distribution efficiency over its rivals, has faced legal action over certain provisions of its distribution agreements. Whether these com-panies crossed the line from competitive advantage to unfair compe-tition and/or monopoly status is not for us to decide, but they clearly illustrate how far competitive advantage can carry an organization.

Of course, Wal-Mart provides an excellent example of competi-tive advantage through superior systems. Their legendary mastery of supply-chain technology changed the retailing landscape in America and now allows them to dictate terms to their suppliers. How powerful is this? Wal-Mart's recent decision to move toward organic grocery products will change the behavior of distributors, farmers, commodities markets, other retailers, and consumers. Interestingly, Wal-Mart's competitive advantage extends into both major categories: lower costs through supply-chain management and clear differentia-tion as the low-price provider of everyday goods.

In general, technology companies cannot sustain competitive advantage unless they constantly reinvent themselves. Even Apple Computer (AAPL), which periodically (and brilliantly) reinvents itself and its products, teeters every few years on the edge of disaster. Still, Apple's frequent phoenix-like resurrection reflects its absolute mastery of product life cycle, whereby they always seem to have a blockbuster product waiting just as an older product loses its luster.

The Best Defense Is to Play Your Own Game

We've always been fond of this quotation from a music book publisher: "We do not compete. We innovate." Truly, the best way to stay consistently profitable is to offer something unique and widely needed. We seek out companies that are genuinely better than their competitors, offering unique benefits if not unique products.

Politicians and other brand-obsessed marketers spend fortunes figuring out how to look better than the competition. As professional investors, it's our duty to find companies that really are better and know how to stay that way. Companies that choose to be different and to celebrate their difference have a much better chance of success in the marketplace.

By definition, a company that consistently generates higher profits than its competitors is said to have competitive advantage. Thus, such companies generally make superior investments.

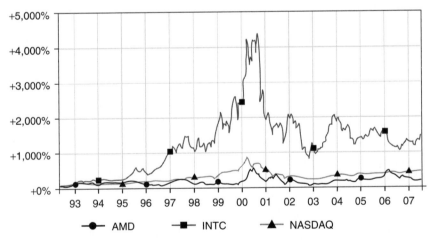

Figure 8.1   Competitive Advantage

Data Source: FT Interactive Data via Capital IQ, a division of Standard & Poor's.

Competitive advantage compares peers, but companies expert in sustaining competitive advantage also tend to outperform the market index over time, as investors reward outstanding performance. In Figure 8.1 we compare microchip powerhouse Intel (INTC) with strong competitor Advanced Micro Devices (AMD). Both produce excellent products, but Intel's momentum, massive R&D investments, and marketing expertise make it very hard to catch, and Wall Street continues to reward this strength.

Although difficult to quantify, competitive advantage must be factored into the value of a company. When Benjamin Graham conceived the margin-of-safety concept, the stock market was reeling from the crash of 1929, and it was relatively easy to find companies selling for less than the value of net assets. Today, such bargains are exceedingly rare, and factors like competitive advantage contribute significantly to an investment's margin of safety.

CHAPTER 9

Company Culture Is More Important than Ever

Sadly, some chief executive officers (CEOs) still exhibit a chilling "ends justify the means" approach to management. But the majority of ineffective leaders display more indifference than cruelty. Their companies suffer because indifference is repaid in kind by coworkers. Sabotage can be discovered and remedied, but mediocre work slips under the radar until the organization fails.

Ultimately, a company's culture will come to reflect the CEO's personality, for better or worse. Hiring is always the most important task in management; hiring the CEO is therefore the single most important decision a company can make. In a film version of *Mutiny on the Bounty*, the British Navy eventually realizes this, as the court-martial judge explains:

> No code can cover all contingencies. We cannot put justice aboard our ships in books. Justice and decency are carried in the heart of the captain, or they be not aboard. It is for this reason that the Admiralty has always sought to appoint its officers from the ranks of gentlemen. The court regrets to note that the appointment of Captain William Bligh was, in that respect, a failure.

Many boards of directors miss the point entirely.

Arrogance Squared Helped HP Lose Its Way

Much has been written about the sacking of Hewlett-Packard (HPQ) CEO Carly Fiorina, and many of her longtime critics exploited the event to vindicate their beliefs and vilify Ms. Fiorina for destroying "The HP Way." We do not believe that Ms. Fiorina was a villain in this scenario. True, she is reputed to be arrogant, dictatorial, and elitist, but that was known by the people who hired her. In fact, these elements of her character were key success factors at her former employers, AT&T and Lucent Technologies (LU), hoary old dinosaurs and strict adherents to the "iron fist" school of management.

Carly Fiorina was exactly what the HP board of directors ordered. Together, they hobbled one of the greatest company cultures in American history. Neither will ever admit to making any mistakes along the way—in itself a mistake when leading a highly educated workforce. But the mistakes they made were very common, and investors should keep a weather eye out for these errors of judgment during any leadership change.

The most critical error is so common that nearly every article about Fiorina's departure reinforced it. Journalists pondered whether she was fired for the company's poor performance or because she damaged the company culture, as if the two were unrelated. We submit that very often, corporate culture is the least appreciated, least understood key success factor for a great company. And we assure you that HP was, and may yet become again, one of the world's great companies.

Culture Matters, Culture Is Real

Prior to hiring Fiorina, the HP board concluded that the company's competitive struggles could be blamed on the company culture. In times of trouble, a very democratic structure is an easy target. One longs for a benign dictator to silence the bickering masses and provide clear direction. It happens to nations, and it happens to companies.

We question whether the board truly understood their own culture; whether the mores, conventions, and commitments of their people had become a mere academic notion to the board, obscured by the very word *culture*, which, after all, is one of the most abused words in business. Some companies use it as code for *racism* or *sexism*, while others use it to excuse a multitude of sins, including a lack of leadership or clear direction.

But when a corporate culture embodies truly noble values and democratic principles, woe befalls those who tamper with it. Hewlett-Packard's culture, first codified in 1957 as their corporate objectives, set the standard and virtually created the concept of corporate culture. As business columnist Jeff Goodell wrote on Salon.com:

> For an entire generation of Silicon Valley entrepreneurs, including Steve Jobs, who has often said that HP was the inspiration for the freewheeling corporate culture at Apple, HP represented the dream of a company that was not just fun to work for and treated its employees well, but which was built upon a foundation of loyalty, trust, and community service. It was the embodiment of ethical capitalism.[1]

Understanding that the board asked Fiorina to change this, we almost feel sympathy for her. Almost—for she approached the task with considerable enthusiasm.

What Is a Company?

We never get tired of saying this: A company is not its machines, nor its buildings, nor its patents, nor its financial statements, nor its ad campaigns. A company is its people. And the people of HP faced a dramatic contrast when Carly Fiorina joined their organization. Whereas the founders of the company practiced an open-door policy, wandered the halls daily, and frequently ate with coworkers in the cafeteria, Fiorina set herself apart. She cloistered herself in an office (or otherwise out of sight); it could take weeks for a coworker to get an appointment to see her. She received a huge and highly publicized compensation package, but still asked the company to move her yacht from the East to the West Coast. And she was not an engineer.

The company went from a bottom-up idea incubator to a top-down "ego-ocracy," in the eyes of tenured employees. Everything was about Carly; she tried to be a rock-star CEO like Steve Jobs, but she lacked Jobs's street credibility. For heaven's sake, Jobs created Apple—twice! His passion for his company and its people is legendary. When Fiorina made herself the star of an ad campaign ostensibly praising the spirit of the company's beloved founders, longtime HP employees felt disingenuousness right through to their bones.

Under Fiorina's rule, the people of HP seemed to lose their voice, and with it their pride. Pride is a great motivator; a good leader helps people find pride in their work. Damage a coworker's compensation and the coworker will certainly complain and might even leave. Damage a coworker's pride and the coworker will seek vengeance.

Give Her an Inch and She Thinks She's a Ruler

Power does not create leaders; good leaders are granted power by those who follow them. Fiorina did not take time to become a leader at HP; rather, she was installed as ruler, and tried to lead through mere authority and sheer force of will. The board ensured an adequate supply of the former, and Fiorina already possessed more than adequate rations of the latter.

During a leadership transition, coworkers are very sensitive, almost brittle. New executives speak the language of transition, but coworkers know when *team player* is just a euphemism for "do what you're told." They also know when "I'm not going to make any drastic changes" means "the layoffs start next month."

Too few executives recognize the most dangerous power their coworkers possess: the power to do mediocre work. If one must battle fierce competition, we'd rather invest in an army of "citizen soldiers," freely and passionately fighting for something they love and following leaders they respect.

Not All Change Is Progress

People have said some pretty harsh things about Carly Fiorina for damaging the HP culture, but we reassert that this is exactly what she was hired to do! Arrogance is an unwillingness to learn from others; the detached yet confident board of directors and their intensely focused CEO were a match made in . . . well, somewhere. We find it sad that companies so often undervalue their own uniqueness. Time and again we hear board members, analysts, and consultants telling entrepreneurial and innovative companies that they need to be more like "real" companies.

Yet when they sacrifice their culture to do so, they make a deal with the devil, trading a chance to be great for a chance to be big, and usually failing. Apple almost lost everything when it chose wrong, but got a very rare second chance through very rare leadership. HP may have an opportunity to reclaim its soul. Perhaps the effort would be helped if the board spent some time considering this section of its corporate objectives:

Employee Commitment

To help HP employees share in the company's success that they make possible; to provide people with employment opportunities based on performance; to create with them a safe, exciting and inclusive work environment that values their diversity and recognizes individual contributions; and to help them gain a sense of satisfaction and accomplishment from their work.[2]

Underlying beliefs supporting this objective:

HP's performance starts with motivated employees; their loyalty is key.

We trust our employees to do the right thing and to make a difference.

Everyone has something to contribute; it's not about title, level or tenure.

An exciting, stimulating work environment is critical to invention.

A diverse workforce gives us a competitive advantage.

Employees are responsible for lifelong learning.

Of course, words are cheap. We want to invest in companies whose actions demonstrate that they take culture seriously, respect their employees, and understand that a great company is more likely to get big than a big company is to get great.

Wall Street was very excited about the selection of Carly Fiorina as CEO of Hewlett-Packard (HPQ) in 1999 (see Figure 9.1). Wall Street was also very excited when she left the company in February 2005. HPQ may never have been a Wall Street darling per se, but the company was consistently profitable and innovative for over 50 years. The board of directors somehow lost hold of the founders' strong sense of company culture, got caught up in the tech boom of the 1990s, and remained disoriented and confused until recently. Despite a new round of scandals and difficulties in 2006, the company seems to regaining some of its former momentum.

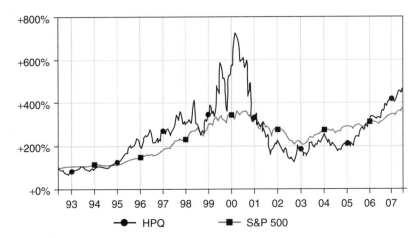

Figure 9.1   A Tale of Two Cultures

Data Source: FT Interactive Data via Capital IQ, a division of Standard & Poor's.

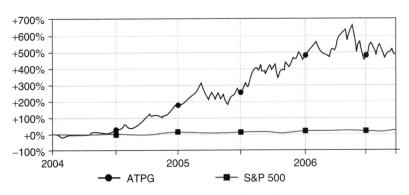

Figure 9.2   A Tale of Two Cultures, continued

Data Source: FT Interactive Data via Capital IQ, a division of Standard & Poor's.

ATP Oil & Gas Corp. (ATPG) understands the importance of teamwork, and created an innovative incentive plan for 2005. (See Figure 9.2.) Upon attainment of company goals, every employee in the company would receive a brand new 2006 Volvo S60. ATP's culture equates big rewards with outstanding performance through alignment of interests. As you can imagine, the company met or exceeded every goal. Based on the graph, do you think this worked out well for shareholder interests?

CHAPTER

10

Bogie and Bergman Explain Elasticity of Demand

Casablanca typically ranks first or second when critics and other film aficionados list their all-time favorite movies. And why not? What other film combines fantastic casting, a moving story, memorable characters, mystery, suspense, music, adventure, romance, *and* three lessons in economics? Naturally, we're attracted to the lessons in economics.

Early in the film, a refugee tries to raise cash by selling her jewelry. "Can't you make it just a little more?" she asks the buyer. He shakes his head. "Diamonds are a drug on the market. Everybody sells diamonds. There are diamonds everywhere." Lesson number one: Excess supply depresses prices.

In the Paris flashback sequence, Ilsa Lund offers Rick Blaine a franc for his thoughts. He replies that in America they'd bring only a penny, and that's all they're worth. "I'm willing to be overcharged," says Ilsa. Lesson two: For nonessential goods, value exists in the mind of the consumer.

Later, after Major Strasser of the Third Reich offers freedom to Victor Laszlo in exchange for the names of resistance leaders throughout Europe, Laszlo says that even if he betrayed his comrades and their enemies killed them all, thousands more would rise up to replace them. Major Strasser responds:

> Herr Laszlo, you have a reputation for eloquence which I can now understand. But in one respect you are mistaken. You said the enemies of the Reich could all be replaced, but there

is one exception. No one could take your place in the event anything unfortunate should occur to you while you were trying to escape.[1]

Lesson number three: Availability of substitutes affects elasticity of demand. When people have alternatives, competition moderates prices. When something, or someone, cannot be replaced, prices climb. In the above scene, Major Strasser understands just how valuable Victor Laszlo is to the resistance because he is irreplaceable.

Casablanca deals with themes of global importance, as Rick points out at the end, ". . . the problems of three little people don't amount to a hill of beans in this crazy world." Economic theory describes "this crazy world," and helps us understand why diamonds are sometimes worthless, how consumer behavior affects prices, and why the fate of the free world might sometimes rest on the shoulders of a single man.

Bananas for Oranges and $$ for Oil

What is economics? In a nutshell, economics is the study of the choices people make in their everyday lives. We have a friend who is just crazy about his health. He always snacks on fruits and vegetables and rarely treats himself to dessert. A few years ago, the price of oranges (his favorite fruit) went through the roof, and he was faced with a decision. Would he pay double the normal price for oranges, or would he switch to apples and bananas? Without much hesitation, he made the switch—keeping his healthy diet and saving some money. Soon after, the demand for oranges fell as more people switched to apples and bananas, and the price of oranges came back down.

Consider another individual, who lived in Ventura, California, and commuted daily to Santa Barbara during the late 1970s and early 1980s. She drove a 1968 American Motors Ambassador, which managed eight miles per gallon of gasoline. In 1978, gasoline cost $0.65 per gallon, and our friend figured the $5 commute was well worth the money she saved by living in Ventura.

To her surprise, the cost of gasoline started to climb, and climb, and climb until one day in 1981 it reached $1.65 per gallon. At this price, our friend calculated that her commute now cost $12.50 per day. She thought to herself: *This is ridiculous. What can I do to cut down on my consumption of gasoline?* She mulled her options and decided that since she didn't know anyone commuting to Santa Barbara and since the cost of living in Santa Barbara was now even higher, her only alternative was to take the bus (which she refused to do).

Elasticity: Simpler than It Sounds

What can we learn about economics from these two friends? Remember, one likes oranges, and the other depends on gasoline. The answer is that people will pay higher prices for oil because they must, but oranges can easily be substituted with bananas. Similarly, people stranded in Death Valley during the middle of summer would gladly spend their life's savings on water if it were in short supply.

This concept is known as *elasticity,* which is the degree to which supply, demand, and price interact. We consider oil demand "inelastic" because changes in its price do not significantly affect the quantity demanded. In addition to gasoline, people depend on oil daily for countless other products such as plastic, pharmaceuticals, asphalt, fertilizer, pesticides, detergents, and paints.

Three-Way Street

Technically, elasticity of demand refers to the degree to which price affects demand and, indirectly, supply. But the three are inextricably linked, particularly when availability is unknown. In the case of oil, we believe prices will continue to be strong for years to come, and we are investing our money accordingly. Consider these factors:

- Demand is growing rapidly in China and India, the world's most populous countries.
- Production capacity cannot be quickly increased, if at all.
- There are no obvious affordable substitutes on the horizon.
- The major source (Middle East) is politically unstable.
- Estimated reserves may be overestimated and difficult to recover.

A very delicate balance exists here. At what price point would gasoline consumption drop? Would that free up supply for growing economies and extend supplies until viable substitutes are developed? Governments and private enterprise walk a tightrope on these issues, and it may be political suicide to focus on the real issue—Americans are gluttonous consumers of oil, and the worst is yet to come.

Today, consumers complain left and right about the outrageous price of gasoline, but in reality it is cheap—too cheap, in our opinion. To put this in perspective, at current prices of $3.15 per gallon, gasoline equates to only $0.39 per pint, which is less than the price of bottled water.

We believe future generations will look back at our time as the "era of petrochemicals." Serious repercussions may result in the world economy if new technologies are not developed in time to bridge the gap between future oil supply and demand. For this reason, we should be asking important questions about our future: What would higher oil prices mean for transportation, consumer spending, interest rates, the value of the dollar, real estate patterns, tourism, world trade, and so on? By investing in select oil production and exploration companies, we are effectively hedging against the possibilities of increasing oil prices, a deep recession, and a declining U.S. dollar-since oil is priced in a world market.

Natural gas provides similar opportunity. Domestic supply is declining in spite of major reinvestment, and demand is increasing for this cleaner-burning fuel. As fears over global warming build, so does natural gas's competitive advantage. Thus, we believe existing reserves will be quite valuable. Uranium and copper are likewise constrained and their demand is inelastic; the price may go up, but the demand will not diminish for the foreseeable future.

But Which Is Better, Elastic or Inelastic Demand?

Readers may assume that we prefer companies that produce products with inelastic demand, but this is not always the case. We are, in a word, opportunistic, so we look for companies that understand and manage the elasticity of their products. Wrigley, for example, brilliantly manages inventory, shelf space, and branding, maintaining fairly consistent profitability despite selling a range of products with highly elastic demand.

Likewise, pharmaceutical companies create inelastic demand for a time with patents, but one must watch the clock and the competition. As soon as the patent runs out, substitutes appear and the supply/demand/price matrix finds a new level of equilibrium at considerably lower margins than when supply was constrained. The best companies manage their product life cycles to maximize profitability, introducing a new, high-margin product just as an older product's margin begins to decline.

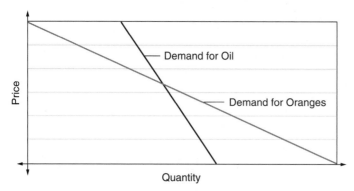

Figure 10.1   Elasticity of Demand

The interrelationship of supply and demand is the easiest and most intuitive concept in economics, often called "the dismal science." Adding the third component of price introduces subtle complexities, particularly when we step out of the realm of the academic (widgets) and into a world where people's lives and livelihoods depend on allocating resources to make the optimal number of refrigerator compressors, or megawatts of electricity, or doses of flu vaccine.

We do not think there is anything "dismal" or dreary about economics. *Casablanca's* Rick Blaine may have felt that the problems of three little people don't amount to a hill of beans in this crazy world, but economic theory describes "this crazy world," and that's important because as Frank Drebin (Leslie Nielsen) explained in the 1988 comedy *The Naked Gun,* "This is our hill, and these are our beans!"[2]

Figure 10.1 is a simplified chart illustrating that price can dramatically influence demand for an easily substituted product like oranges, while demand for oil varies mildly in response to price changes. Supply, demand, and price are each affected by a range of external factors. A mild winter reduces the demand for heating oil and natural gas, for example. The extreme hurricane season of 2005 and milder-than-expected hurricane season of 2006 wreaked havoc on oil and gas prices, as did political tensions throughout the Middle East. However, Americans' driving habits hardly changed at all during 2006, even though gas prices rose dramatically through the year before declining slightly in the fall. Because of the relative inelasticity of gasoline, the rising monthly expenditures for fuel eventually reverberate into more elastic consumables, as people divert grocery, clothing, and entertainment money to pay their gasoline bills.

CHAPTER

11

Red Flags and Roaches

Setting Standards for What *Not* to Buy

We recommend small, manageable portfolios of 10 to 12 stocks, but even if you decide to hold 100 or 200 stocks, they will represent a very small fraction of the available public companies. In other words, *not* buying stocks is the more common "activity," even for the most active investor. Know the red flags that help you determine which stocks not to buy, for this skill serves you every day in the market.

"Stocks I'd Avoid" is one of our favorite chapters in one of our favorite books, Peter Lynch's *One Up on Wall Street* (Penguin, 1989). As portfolio manager, Lynch guided Fidelity's Magellan Fund from $20 million to $14 *billion*, making it the best-performing fund in the world during his 13-year tenure.

Because of our commitment to long-term results, we share many of Lynch's beliefs, particularly those about stocks to avoid. In fact, the most common result of our relentless research is the decision to pass; we go looking for trouble, and when we find it, we walk away. Lynch offers useful advice on broad categories of stocks to question, and we gladly share some of them with you here.

Hot Stocks Often Flame Out

Lynch opens the chapter with the stock most loathed: ". . . the hottest stock in the hottest industry, the one that gets the most favorable publicity, the one that every investor hears about in the car pool or on the commuter train." In most cases, such stocks rise very quickly and fall even more quickly. He compares such stocks with a roulette spin, and we agree. As we've stated in the past, West Coast Asset Management does not play the market for "quick scores." We prefer to invest in companies likely to produce long-term capital appreciation.

Hot Air Doesn't Pay Dividends

Certain types of positive publicity, or "buzz," about a company actually serve as signals to steer clear; one must not disregard proven measures of value and business acumen just because of hype. Lynch cites "the next something" as a stock to beware. Of course, this is true beyond the stock market; how many "next Michael Jordans" have we heard about in the past 15 years? When a company is touted as the next Microsoft or the next FedEx, promoters are asking us to use our imagination *instead* of our good sense. Investing requires imagination *and* good sense. Don't fall for their hyperbolic sales pitches.

Pride Cometh before Absurd Acquisitions

If we didn't already respect and admire Peter Lynch, his coining of the term *diworsification* would have won us over. In his words, "Instead of buying back shares or raising dividends, profitable companies often prefer to blow the money on foolish acquisitions." This is so common that we don't know whether to laugh or cry. Watch out for executives whose hubris convinces them they can manage a far-flung empire, regardless of how diverse the products or services.

Jack Welch took draconian measures to reduce the number of businesses General Electric was in, but they still have far too many unrelated units, subsidized by the financial machinations of GE Capital. What synergy exists between their aircraft engine manufacturing business, their medical systems business, and their television network? We are wary of these overcomplicated behemoths.

Big Secrets Are Often Big Embarrassments

"Whisper stocks" earn a place on Lynch's list, and who among us has not been pulled aside by a friend to hear about the long shot that might just hit it big? Lynch pegs the appeal of these "whizbang stories."

Often the whisper companies are on the brink of solving the latest National problem: the oil shortage, drug addiction, AIDS. The solution is either (a) very imaginative, or (b) impressively complicated.

He goes on to cite examples that will have you rolling on the floor laughing—if you didn't lose a bundle on them. These stocks generate buzz through an emotionally compelling story. The companies usually have no earnings or profits, escaping traditional measures of value. Sounds like a lot of dot-coms in the 1990s, doesn't it?

Real Trends Don't Rush You

The average investor, like most people, likes to follow trends. Who wants to be left out of something new and exciting? Who wants to miss out on what everybody else is talking about? From dot-coms to theme restaurants to miracle cures, investors have found numerous ways to lose money by letting their emotions overrule their commitment to business fundamentals.

Real trends create multiple opportunities over time. Rather than rush onto the ground floor of an unknown, we'd rather get in on the third or fifth or tenth floor of a company that has proven its building skills.

Cockroach Theory Warns of Trouble to Come

When studying a company, we sometimes uncover a cockroach. And there's no such thing as "just one cockroach." That sentence pretty much sums up cockroach theory in the stock market.

Many investors wrestle with this quandary: The price looks right, the market is good, the management seems sound, but the company has just announced a Securities and Exchange Commission (SEC) investigation, or a group of shareholders has just announced a lawsuit, or there's something slightly peculiar about its accounting methods. Sometimes a company issues more shares of stock for no apparent reason, or there's a subtle but consistent erosion of its earnings, or inventory levels are growing or consistently being written off.

Alone, each may seem like a small problem. The company's public relations experts insist that the little problem means nothing, but each of these caveats represents a cockroach to us, and as we said, there is no such thing as just one cockroach.

Inevitably, a bright light cast upon these companies will set other cockroaches scurrying. For example, at one time we were looking at Pre-Paid Legal (PPD). In effect, it sells attorney services for a flat monthly fee. Generally, we like a business with recurring revenue streams, no inventory, good growth, and the good sense to repurchase stock when it can. Pre-Paid Legal met these criteria.

But there were questions about its accounting methods, so we held back. The SEC later investigated Pre-Paid and determined it did not properly expense its advance commissions. As a result, Pre-Paid reissued its financial statements and severed ties with Deloitte & Touche, its longtime auditor. Throughout this drama, the stock dropped like a rock. While it's true that the market tends to overreact to bad news, we have a responsibility to factor that overreaction into our buying decisions.

Cockroaches Cause Knee-Jerk Reaction for Some

We also factor cockroaches into our selling decisions. We know the dangers of excessive trading and the virtue of long-term commitment to quality companies in growing industries. But stock purchases do not require a vow of "until death do you part." Cockroaches, in the form of management malfeasance, or any other significant surprise, can motivate us to sell, although we are not as quick to sell as some.

Profiled in a 2000 issue of *Stockhouse Financial News*, Pat McHugh, then manager of the $120 million Global Strategy Canadian Companies mutual fund, explained that he sells at the first negative surprise. "We are firm believers in the cockroach theory of investing," McHugh says. "You see a company with one earnings surprise and you haven't seen them all. It will be followed by a series of subsequent negative surprises."

Don't confuse an "earnings surprise" with headlines about a company missing Wall Street expectations by a cent or two. We consider the entire idea of "earnings guidance" suspect; we compare a company's performance to our expectations, not Wall Street's. Seriously, the idea that gigantic multidivision, multinational companies like General Electric can somehow meet earnings projections to the penny strikes us as ludicrous. Of course, Enron was quite good at meeting projections.

In any case, mutual fund manager McHugh has different goals than separate accounts managers like West Coast Asset Management. Yes, we are wary of cockroaches discovered in our holdings, but other factors, like tax efficiency, also play an important role in the decision to sell stocks.

Note: We sell any company whose management has engaged in misleading or unethical practices; companies are made of people, and the people at the top set the culture. We also watch out for management that simply cannot execute their plans, the "gonna-do" companies that never quite get it done.

Gonna-Do Companies Often Don't

Experience trains one to be mindful of patterns. Our experience in business, real estate, and stock investing leads us to the conclusion that good companies get better, the mediocre stay mediocre, and the bad tend to get worse. Often, a company that has fallen on hard times but seems full of potential tempts us. Unfortunately, time and again we see such companies 2, 5, or 10 years later, and they are just as full of unrealized potential. They present compelling plans but cannot deliver.

When we were kids, conventional wisdom held that in the event of a nuclear holocaust, only cockroaches and Twinkies would survive. Sounds like a bit of a cockroach heaven, really. Since cockroaches thrive in dark and messy environments, the cockroach theory metaphor again reinforces our preference for simple, transparent companies that don't require us to crawl under cabinets to see every nook and cranny of their financial statements.

Newell's (NWL) 1999 acquisition of Rubbermaid presents a clear example of "diworsification." Known for acquiring small, troubled companies and turning them around, Newell broke with their own tradition to acquire a big company that was doing well (see Figure 11.1). Then they did what they do best: They turned it around! A former coworker at Newell told us, "It didn't fit our model, but the guys just wanted it."

The Standard & Poor's October 31, 2006, stock report on NWL had this to say:

> In our opinion, NWL has struggled since its acquisition of Rubbermaid in 1999 to resume a consistent pattern of growth in revenues and earnings. From 1999 to 2005, revenues were down, although three years had up sales . . . Under the new leadership beginning in October 2005, we think that NWL should be able to improve upon the 8.5% operating margin achieved in 2005,

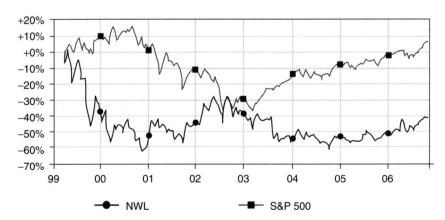

Figure 11.1   Newell Rubbermaid Diworsification

Data Source: FT Interactive Data via Capital IQ, a division of Standard & Poor's.

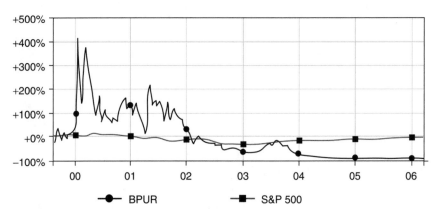

Figure 11.2   Biopure, the "Next Big Thing"

Data Source: FT Interactive Data via Capital IQ, a division of Standard & Poor's

although we don't expect it to get back to the pre-Rubbermaid level of better than 15%.[1]

At the turn of this century, Biopure looked like the "next big thing," thanks to its synthetic blood, an innovation that could revolutionize trauma centers and emergency rooms. Investors rushed to get in on the ground floor, but many ended up in the basement (see Figure 11.2).

Keep in mind that while Biopure may have an important, valuable, lifesaving product, a company must be valued based on facts, not hopes. Excited investors may have hurt this company more than any research-and-development hurdles it faced.

Of course, nearly every dot-com company is an example of hype overcoming rational thought. Hucksters promoted the "new economy" and suckers bought it, just as they have since the 1600s, when tulip mania gripped the Netherlands, and tulip bulbs traded at valuations exceeding the average annual income.

CHAPTER

12

Inspirational Figures: David Packard

A coin toss gave David Packard second billing on his company's logo, but his contributions to American business, industry, and society are second to none. And make no mistake: *contribution* was the keyword in Packard's life. Lauded for his technical expertise, administrative skills, philanthropy, and leadership, Packard possessed a rare and valuable trait from an early age: wisdom. This wisdom manifested itself in two lifelong attributes: a willingness to learn and a desire to give.

In 1989, the State of California designated the garage in which Hewlett-Packard was launched as a historical landmark, and declared it the birthplace of Silicon Valley. But Packard's influence extends far beyond the technological and economic successes of northern California's computer dynasty. With partner Bill Hewlett, Packard contributed significantly to the twentieth century's rapid advancement of science and engineering, at the same time reinventing the art of business management.

Energetic Beginnings

In 1912, David Packard was born to an attorney father and high school teacher mother in Pueblo, Colorado, which was still very much a "Wild West" town. Roaming the prairie and the downtown streets with equal curiosity, Packard's boyhood was filled with hunting, fishing, school athletics, and "scientific" experiments, usually involving explosives—at least until he discovered radio, which led to his interest in electronics.

While competing on the basketball and track teams in high school, Packard absorbed the advice that he later credited as "a guiding principle in developing and managing at HP. Get the best people, stress the importance of teamwork, and get them fired up to win the game."

Enrolling at Stanford University in 1930, Packard met two very influential men: fellow student and future partner Bill Hewlett, and professor, mentor, and all-around supporter Fred Terman. It was Terman who most encouraged Hewlett and Packard to go into business.

Lessons from the Factory Floor

Upon graduation in 1934, Packard accepted a position with General Electric in Schenectady, New York. While problem-solving a quality control issue—large rectifier tubes kept exploding—Packard learned a valuable lesson. "It soon became apparent that the instructions the engineering department gave the factory people were not adequate to ensure that every step would be done properly. . . . That was a very important lesson for me—that personal communication was often necessary to back up written instructions. That was the genesis of what became 'management by walking around' at the Hewlett-Packard Company." Thereafter, unlike most engineers, Packard spent a lot of his time on the factory floor.

In 1938, Packard got married, returned to California, and pursued his master's degree in electrical engineering at Stanford. In 1939, he and Bill Hewlett launched the Hewlett-Packard Company in the garage of Packard's home in Palo Alto. Capitalized with a little over $500, the two found that Hewlett's circuit design skills and Packard's mastery of manufacturing processes made them a powerful team. Moreover, they both possessed a strong work ethic and the natural curiosity of lifelong learners.

"In those early days Bill and I had to be versatile. We had to tackle almost everything ourselves—from inventing and building products to pricing, packaging, and shipping them; from dealing with customers and sales representatives to keeping the books; from writing the ads to sweeping up at the end of the day. Many of the things I learned in this process were invaluable and not available in business schools."

Why a Company Exists

In the foreword to the 2005 edition of David Packard's *The HP Way* (HarperCollins), Jim Collins wrote, "Most entrepreneurs pursue the question 'How can I succeed?' From day one, Packard and Hewlett pursued a different question: 'What can we contribute?' and thereby HP attained extraordinary success."

HP designed and built electronic test and measuring instruments, and went on to develop pocket calculators and mini-computers, and to lead the world in computer printing technology. Their amazing success owed less to Hewlett's and Packard's individual skills than to their shared vision: whatever they sold couldn't just be new; it had to be better, and it had to contribute to a client's success. They viewed profit as a result, not an objective in and of itself.

In 1949, Packard shocked a meeting of fellow business leaders by suggesting, as Collins wrote, "A company has a responsibility beyond making a profit for stockholders; it has a responsibility to recognize the dignity of its employees as human beings, to the well-being of its customers, and to the community at large." No one at the meeting supported this point of view. They thought he was a freak.

In the pursuit of this vision, HP engineered a new kind of company.

Management by Objective

David Packard may have done more than anyone to shatter the old "command and control" model of management, recognizing that highly talented individuals respond poorly to snapped orders. Rather, Packard saw that teamwork could come from an alignment of interests, encouraging each player to direct his or her best abilities to the betterment of the team. Thus was born the concept of management by objective, wherein the leadership of the company establishes the guiding principles of the organization, the coworkers themselves create a culture to support these principles, and the leaders in turn nurture the culture.

In 1957, Packard, Hewlett, and 20 of their managers met in Sonoma, California, and established a set of corporate objectives. "We thought that if we could get everybody to agree on what our objectives were and to understand what we were trying to do, then we could turn them loose and they would move in a common direction." The corporate objectives described the company's approach toward profit, customers, field of interest, growth, employees, organization, and citizenship, but said nothing about markets, technology, hierarchy, or competition. They simply laid the groundwork for a culture that, unlike most corporate environments of the time, encouraged both independence and teamwork.

Contributions to the Art of Management

David Packard and Bill Hewlett's approach to management bequeathed many gifts to today's managers and their teams. *Management by objective*, for example, empowered individuals to be creative problem solvers. Not only does the process create an organic and self-sustaining kind of teamwork, but it prevents *diworsification* for companies, which can stay focused on what they do best and what fits their core competencies.

Likewise, *management by walking around* improves communication, quality, teamwork, and profits. Hewlett's and Packard's visible presence and easy availability (they insisted on a companywide open-door policy, believing that interruptions were a small price to pay for the advantages of open and frank communication with the talented people they hired) earned them deep credibility with their coworkers. A drill press operator on the outskirts of the factory knew that the CEO and president understood what he did and appreciated his contribution.

Flextime was another fascinating—and revolutionary—innovation of "The HP Way." As Packard explained, "To my mind, flextime is the essence of respect for and trust in people. It says that we both appreciate that our people have busy personal lives and that we trust them to devise, with their supervisor and work group, a schedule that is personally convenient yet fair to others."

Packard also saw that the future of industry was a future of learning. One illustrative invention was the Honors Cooperative Program: "The program made it possible for us to hire top-level young graduates from around the country with the promise that if they came to work for us and we thought it appropriate, they could attend graduate school while on full HP salary. Originally, the company paid part of their tuition as well, and more recently has paid all of their tuition. More than 400 HP engineers have obtained master's or doctorate degrees through this program. It has enabled us to hire the top engineering graduates from universities all across the country for a number of years—an important factor in the ultimate success of our company."

A Well-Engineered Business

Many leaders claim to appreciate the value of talent in their organization, but Packard also seemed to understand the *nature* of talent. Rather than engineer their company to use people like replaceable parts, Packard and Hewlett respected their employees. They refused, for example, to pursue boom-and-bust contract work because they did not want to go through cycles of hiring and then laying people off. They wanted the kind of contribution only loyalty can produce, so they modeled loyalty to their workers.

In 1970, when the economy stumbled and the company faced layoffs, Packard proposed—and the company embraced—a novel alternative. Rather than lay off 10 percent of the workforce, the entire company took a 10 percent work schedule cut, working just nine days every two weeks. "The net result of this program was that effectively all shared the burden of the recession, good people were not released into a very tough job market, and we had our highly qualified workforce in place when business improved." Packard hastened to point out that this solution applied only to what was clearly a temporary situation; the company could not guarantee full employment under all scenarios.

Contributions beyond the Workplace

David Packard became very wealthy through the success of Hewlett-Packard, and his commitment "to meet the obligations of good citizenship by making contributions to the community and to the institutions in our society which generate the environment in which we operate" extended far beyond his work life.

Packard served for three years as Deputy Secretary of Defense under Melvin Laird in the Nixon White House. He and Hewlett donated generously to Stanford University and many local and national charities. In 1978, Packard and his wife Lucile created the Monterey Bay Aquarium Foundation, which in 1984 opened the Monterey Bay Aquarium, one of the most innovative, educational, and beautiful aquariums in the world. The Lucile Salter Packard Children's Hospital at Stanford University opened in 1991.

A Legacy of Inspiration

Steve Jobs credited Hewlett-Packard's culture as the inspiration for Apple Computer's creative approach to engineering and management. In fact, when Jobs left Apple under duress in the 1980s, his first impulse was to apologize to David Packard.

When David Packard died on March 26, 1996, his legacy was visible in three great accomplishments: a very successful company, an effective philanthropic foundation, and, most important of all, the enduring love of family, friends, and coworkers. These, then, represent the fruits of the contribution-driven life.

PART

III

THE OWNER'S MANUAL

Visit the trading floor of a stock or commodities exchange and you will find strange people, speaking a language bearing little resemblance to any spoken outside the walls. Of course, you notice that only after you get over the shock of witnessing the screaming, flailing, heads-about-to-explode traders in action. Every field has its own nomenclature, and investing is no different. Prospective investors face a deluge of information about investing, but one does not need an advanced accounting degree to understand most of the numbers and ideas that should influence investment decisions. This section covers the basics:

- When evaluating advice, consider the source.
- A financial statement is more likely to inspire questions than to answer them.
- See beyond the marketing pizzazz of annual reports.
- Learn to interpret the many meanings of "inventory."
- Try these 10 quick tests of a company's strength.

CHAPTER 13

Televised Advice: No Worse than Drilling Your Own Teeth

Years ago, the *Second City Television (SCTV)* comedy show featured a sketch promoting a home dentistry kit. "Since you're not licensed to give yourself shots of Novocain," explains the host, "substitute shots of tequila." He then consumes mass quantities of tequila and, using drills and mirrors, drunkenly fills his own cavities, with periodic screams of pain.

Many people take the same approach to investing, except that instead of tequila, they numb themselves with mass quantities of "expert" advice from books, web pages, newspapers, radio, and television talk shows. Then they invest, with periodic screams of pain.

We have no doubt that most people possess the intelligence to manage their own investments; as this book demonstrates, the concepts are simple. But most people lack the time, discipline, and emotional detachment necessary for effective investing, so they seek shortcuts in the guise of actionable advice. It has been reported that stocks featured on Jim Cramer's *Mad Money* television show increase in price soon after the show, only to retreat within a few days. This suggests that a number of people are acting impulsively on televised investment advice. The popular investment advice out there, despite generally good quality, is no substitute for personal, professional investment advice.

Guilty Pleasure

Over the years, television's attempts to cover business and investing have ranged from the wry, thoughtful wit of the late Louis Rukeyser to the manic, *Pee-wee's Playhouse* approach of Cramer. Generally, television cannot afford the time to study any issue in depth, and equity investing is no exception. Moreover, the programming needs of television imbue most investing shows with an anxiety-inducing need to present something new every day. This leads many viewers to the very bad habit of excessive trading.

This is no surprise. The average investor, managing his or her own portfolio, operates in a trade-obsessed universe. Online and discount brokerages promote the cost of trades as their primary selling point. There is a lot more to investing than trading, but trading is a key source of revenue on Wall Street, a conflict of interest left over from the days when giant stockbrokers roamed the earth.

Much of the information reaching investors emphasizes the mechanics of buying and selling stock based on trends of the market. Products and services for investors are biased toward this technical analysis of price trends rather than fundamental analysis of a company's value. It's useful information, but it's no substitute for an investment philosophy and process. It's also no substitute for hands-on research. Opportunities come in different shapes and sizes and are often missed by investors unwilling to kick the tires or get their hands dirty.

Commanders, Teachers, and Mentors

Money magazine editor-at-large Jean Chatzky wrote in her June 26, 2006, column, ". . . experts screaming about your money may make for good TV, but it doesn't always work one-on-one."[1] She pointed out that television personalities like Jim Cramer and Suze Orman are "part of a recent American fascination with being told just how wrong we are, by the likes of Simon Cowell, Judge Judy, and Ann Coulter."

One expert interviewed by Chatzky suggests there are two primary types of financial advisers: commanders and teachers. Commanders, which include aggressive shouters like Cramer and Orman, tell you what to do and expect you to do it with no questions asked. Teachers, on the other hand, walk you through the process and attempt to ensure your understanding. Teachers are considered the superior choice, but Chatzky concedes that commanders are popular because their style simply works better for some people.

We consider ourselves a hybrid of the two types: a mentor. Because we manage our clients' assets with discretion, we have control over investments. However, we strive to ensure that clients understand what we are doing and why. Thus, we can act quickly when opportunity arises, but we also prepare clients to make better choices themselves—and, frankly, to better appreciate the choices we make.

Professional financial advisers must assume the role of teacher or commander as needed. As one colleague told us, "Some clients, especially institutions, are looking for a particular expertise and they just want trouble-free, expert execution. On the other hand, you always bring knowledge to the table, and the clients who thirst for a better understanding of investing appreciate it. It builds loyalty, because when you can shed light on a complicated subject, people remember where they learned it."

Simple Concepts, Difficult Execution

Warren Buffett's extremely successful investing style requires deep knowledge of a company before funds are committed, and his new investments make news because they are so infrequent. Consider the research required to know a company's assets (including potentially under- or overvalued real estate; for example, there are railroads and oil companies that own massive tracts of land that have been on their books for decades, at the original price!), whether the stock price is a bargain (understanding the present value of future cash flows, with all the assumptions that entails), and what potential catalysts might cause the stock price to increase (supply and demand; Food and Drug Administration approvals; new patents; social, political, demographic changes). As we often say, investing is simple, but not easy.

But in one interview, Jim Cramer is quoted as saying, "I follow about 1,000 stocks closely, and there's another 500 or 1,000 I keep an eye on."[2] Closely? Maybe Cramer means he follows the stock price closely. On the show, dozens of stocks are mentioned, and he has an opinion on every one. But where's the expertise? Does he really know all the underlying information on the company, or does he just have an opinion on the price?

It's hard for us to imagine knowing more than 1,000 companies in great enough detail to understand the margin of safety, discount to intrinsic value, potential risks, and probable catalysts. We are aware of many companies that we would love to buy at the right price, but only a handful are under serious consideration at any given time. When the price of a company on our watch list drops significantly, we are able to quickly reassess our understanding of the business and act nimbly to take advantage of the opportunity. This is long-term, time-consuming work. There's no "lightning round" for entrepreneurial investors.

Consider the Source

Many wealthy Americans are entrepreneurs who made their fortunes through hard work in specific businesses; few are financial experts. Thus, like the average investor, they rely on professionals for advice. Blessed with a bumper crop of professionals offering such advice, it's important to remember what profession they are in: Are they investment advisers or entertainers?

A professional financial adviser makes it his or her job to know you, your financial situation, your risk tolerance, your time frame, and your goals before offering advice. Books, Web sites, and television personalities cannot know these things.

With over 6,000 personal finance books in print, hundreds of Web sites, and even round-the-clock television networks devoted to finance and investing, there is no shortage of advice out there. Of course, one person's great advice could be another person's invitation to disaster. You need a personal investing strategy, one that incorporates your individual needs and goals.

Educator and entrepreneur Brian Bemel organizes the annual Village of Tales Storytelling Festival in Ojai, California, and in 2006 he opened the proceedings with a reminder about why storytellers still matter in our media-saturated world. He said that a few years ago, a village in Africa received the wonderful gift of electricity. Soon, television sets filled every hut. But just a year later, a visiting anthropologist discovered the television sets dumped at the edge of the village. The anthropologist was confused, so he inquired of the chief:

"Why don't you use your television sets?"

"We have a storyteller," said the chief.

"But the television knows thousands of stories," said the anthropologist.

"That's true," replied the chief, "but the storyteller knows us."

Margin of safety is a critical concept of investing, but one rarely discussed on television (see Figure 13.1). As this simplified diagram illustrates, two companies with a market cap of $100 million and a stock price of $20 may appear to cost the same. But the person who invests in company A gets the cash and real estate, in effect paying only $50 million for the $100 million company. An investor in company B, however, pays $100 million and takes on an additional $50 million in debt. Company A provides a greater "margin of safety" because in a worst-case scenario, one's investment does not drop to zero.

Moreover, company A has greater flexibility to use its cash or take on debt for acquisitions, research and development, and other opportunities. Also, while company B could be destroyed by any significant trouble (economic downturn or natural disaster), company A is better positioned to weather such storms.

Margin of safety is the entrepreneurial investor's answer to the question, "What is the worst that could happen?" Warren Buffett's number one rule of investing is "Never Lose Money," so margin of safety is therefore a very high priority. In a best-case—and very rare—scenario, one finds a stock selling for less than the company's

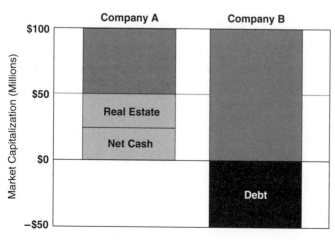

Figure 13.1   Margin of Safety

net tangible asset value, in which case one could lose money only through extraordinary circumstances.

This concept is not difficult, but the margin of safety must be individually analyzed for each prospective investment, vis-à-vis the goals and risk tolerance of each investor. Television cannot provide this level of depth and customization.

14

Lies, Damned Lies, and Financial Statements

It was no surprise that many other problems appeared once a bright light was shone on Enron's accounting irregularities. Awakened by the mighty crash of Enron's collapse, investors and regulators began closely examining the accounting practices of other companies, too.

Under this overdue scrutiny, stock prices fell, bankruptcies multiplied, jobs were lost, and retirement savings evaporated. The damage to companies paled against the damaged confidence of coworkers and investors worldwide.

Financial obfuscation is not new, but has certainly reached new heights of absurdity in the public markets during the past 15 years. For one's own protection, an entrepreneurial investor must know how to read a financial statement. To that end, we offer our usual advice: *simplify!*

By definition, public companies must parade their results before the public, and they do so in the form of a financial statement. Like the fabled emperor, companies want to look their best when they appear in public, so they put a lot of effort into dressing up their financial statements. Some wish to show off their fine physique, earned through long hours at the gym. Others wish to hide some subtle imperfection. Still others want to disguise their true selves. You may recall that the emperor was tricked into wearing nothing— and his subjects accepted this because they were told he was wearing a suit of fabric so fine that only the finest people could see it. In this context, knowing how to read a financial statement can bring a whole new meaning to *transparency* in business.

Rich or Poor, It's Good to Have Money

Most personal and small-business bookkeeping software is based on the familiar model of the checkbook, and for good reason. No matter how we complicate our financial lives with investments and loans and tax strategies, our checkbook answers a very important question: Have we got any money? That's why we begin our study of a company's finances with the cash flow statement and balance sheet.

We're keenly interested in understanding a company's sources and uses of cash flow. We also focus intensely on a company's assets, net of debt, separating those that could be sold in a liquidation, and those that do not support the underlying business and could be sold to repurchase stock or pay dividends. This provides a basis for quantifying margin of safety and identifying hidden assets. What is the value of a company's cash and equivalents, receivables, inventory, marketable securities, manufacturing machinery, land, buildings, and so on?

But the process really begins with this simple question: At the end of the year, is there more or less cash in the company's bank account? If there is less, where did it go? If there is more, where did it come from? We study the inventory level, accounts payable, and accounts receivable to see which is rising, which is falling, and why.

Rising inventories indicate potential risk, because it's easy to get stuck with outdated merchandise, particularly technology, fashion, perishables, or fad products. If cash seems to be turning into accounts receivable, there is also rising risk because you can get stuck with bad debt. All in all, if we're going to get stuck with anything, we prefer cash.

Consider a musical instrument retailer; we often see ads for expensive guitars with no money down and no payments for 12 months. The company gets to book the sales and profits up front, so it might show increased earnings but negative cash flow and increasing receivables. There's an old joke that the difference between a musician and a large pizza is the fact that a large pizza can feed a family of four. Is a company that provides easy credit for such goods a prudent investment?

The Bottom Line Is Not Always the Bottom Line

Some numbers paraded as key indicators are not as important as they might seem. "Earnings," for example, is simply too easy to manipulate under Generally Accepted Accounting Principles.

The January 24, 2002, *Wall Street Journal* suggested two red flags that illustrate the unreliability of earnings as a credible measure of performance. One is the source of earnings; many public companies rely on multiple sources of revenue, and these must be examined and compared. Consider General Electric's disproportionate dependence on GE Capital's profits. A company with numerous manufacturing divisions, GE derives much of its profits from its finance division. We lack confidence in this unbalanced approach, particularly during any kind of economic volatility.

Another red flag mentioned in the article: "recurring nonrecurring charges." The paper quotes Nathaniel Guild from the Short ALERT Web site, who declares, "You can write off anything, in any fashion. There is very little regulation in that area." Thus, we notice companies that seem to reorganize and restructure nearly every year, writing off the charges as "one-time" expenses.

Thus, "earnings," which should be the most important line in a financial report, often represents little more than wishful thinking or outright misrepresentation.

Accounting Crisis or Accounting Culture?

Often, managers and executives find both their tenure and their compensation tied directly to the price of their stock. Investors determine the stock price, and investors are influenced by the information made available to them in financial statements. Rule bending, exaggeration, and manipulation seem like an accounting crisis, but really represent accounting culture in fiercely competitive markets. According to *Wall Street Journal* deputy editor David Wessel, "Too many companies treat accounting rules the way they treat the tax laws: If it isn't expressly forbidden, it's okay."

Some companies change their accounting policies to make their numbers look better. They adopt whatever rules suit them best, regardless of the stage of the game. Companies disclose these changes in the footnotes of their financial statements, and you can bet that such disclosures activate our cockroach radar. (Remember that a "cockroach" is any negative discovery about a company, so called because there is no such thing as one cockroach.)

Why Cash Flow Is King

Cash flow is the lifeblood of a business. A healthy company has cash flowing freely throughout it. Excess cash flow means liquidity and flexibility, allowing the company to explore ever-wider options.

Most Wall Street analysts use earnings as a primary measure of valuation. This is no surprise, since these same analysts recommended Enron, WorldCom, and other famous disasters. The smart money pays attention to cash flow and how it is being managed.

While income statements can be cloaked in mystery, the cash flow statement has no "drama queen" personality and wears no makeup; it is what it is. We can easily see how much cash is generated by the company's operating activities, and we can see how they spend it. Some managers maximize cash flow and distribute it efficiently through new projects, share repurchases, and dividend payments, while others waste cash on terrible acquisitions and careless extravagance.

Generally, young, growing companies maximize the return on their excess cash by reinvesting in the business to increase profits and raise shareholder value. Maturing companies, however, might reinvest only a portion, then pay shareholder dividends or repurchase shares with the remainder. Mature companies cannot grow as rapidly as young companies and, therefore, reinvest less into the company while returning the rest to shareholders.

Spin Doctor, Heal Thyself

Whatever fancy footwork and sleight of hand companies might use to overcomplicate their financial statements, two numbers on the balance sheet tend to be real.

The first is "cash and equivalents." *Equivalents* refers to any company assets that can be converted to cash immediately, including securities that mature within 90 days. We already explained the importance of cash; this line tells you exactly how much is available.

The second number that tends to be true is *sales*. It's not that companies don't sometimes try to fudge the sales number; it's that they usually get caught because the number is easily verifiable. Brazen misrepresentation of sales, such as Enron's use of "mark-to-market"

Jake's Toy Store   BALANCE SHEET
Palm Springs, California
December 31, 2001

Cash	$100,000	Accounts Payable	$250,000
Inventory (*Note 1*)	$200,000		
Current Assets	$300,000	Current Liabilities	$250,000
Land & Building (*Note 2*)	$100,000	Mortgage on Property (*Note 2*)	$200,000
Total Assets	$400,000	Total Liabilities	$450,000
		Equity	($50,000)
			$400,000

Jake's Toy Store Income Statement January 1 - December 31, 2001		1. What is the current ratio?
		2. What is the inventory turn?
Sales	$1,000,000	3. What is the debt-to-equity ratio?
Cost of Sales	$500,000	4. What is the break-even point?
Operating Costs	$300,000	
		5. What do you think are the problems and opportunities for the owner?
Net Income	$200,000	

Note 1: LIFO Method (Last In First Out)
Note 2: Land and Building Purchased in 1949 - Refinanced in 1981

Figure 14.1   Jake's Toy Store, Part 1

accounting, will not stand up to a serious look at cash flow. In the case of the musical instrument retailer mentioned earlier, the rising level of accounts receivable alerts us to question the sales number. However complicated the business, sales minus costs equals profit. Sales grow, stay flat, or shrink. A company's sales tell much of its story.

Executives, accountants, and consultants often overcomplicate financial statements to hide bad news and exaggerate good news, rather than present a forthright accounting of the company's performance. One wonders what would happen if they put as much energy into improving performance as they put into obscuring it.

Why Is the Emperor Shivering?

They say that experience is a harsh teacher because the lesson comes after the test. Benjamin Disraeli—the British prime minister who allegedly declared, "There are three kinds of lies: lies, damned lies, and statistics"—suffered enormous investment losses early in his career. He learned from his experience to question the statistics presented by others. Experience is truly an effective teacher, but learning from other people's experience is far less painful.

One of the reasons we invest in simple companies and industries is that their financial statements are easier to understand. Businesses succeed when they provide value and control costs, not because of artful financial statements. Financial statement analysis is dispassionate work. Study the sources and uses of cash as if you were reviewing your own finances. Don't fall for hype, spin-doctoring, and excuses. Experience suggests that if the emperor looks naked, it's because he isn't wearing any clothes.

Take a look at the financial statement for Jake's Toy Store (see Figure 14.1). Based on the information available, can you answer the questions? Does this seem like a good investment? We'll discuss this further at the end of Chapter 16.

CHAPTER

15

How to Be an Annual Report Detective

The turning point in the 1993 blockbuster film *The Fugitive* comes as U.S. Marshal Sam Gerard reads pharmaceutical giant Devlin MacGregor's annual report. "This company's a monster," says Gerard, realizing that someone other than Dr. Richard Kimble may have had a motive for murder.[1]

Dramatic? Well, it's only a movie. But a company's annual report could be the turning point for a prospective investor as well, since the document holds clues to the company's culture, positioning, profitability, stability, competition, and long-term growth potential.

Investors should read annual reports and proxy statements with skepticism, because these documents often hold hidden meaning. Inspired by Matt Krantz's "How to Read an Annual Report" article in the February 24, 2004, issue of *USA Today*, we offer our own hints, tips, and tricks for decoding these common—yet often inscrutable—documents.[2]

Know What an Annual Report Is Not

Unlike the regulation-defined 10-K document that every public company must file with the Securities and Exchange Commission (SEC), the annual report usually offers fewer details and more flash. The 10-K filing follows a very strict structure, but annual reports may be as unique as the companies they represent.

Because the annual report is not the whole story of the company, it's a good idea to review everything you already know (or think you know) about the company before you open the document. Also, it is not a book (although some include very entertaining fiction), so one need not read it from beginning to end. In fact, we recommend starting at the end.

Interview the Witnesses

The auditor's report, usually tucked away in the back of the annual report, offers the opinion of independent accountants who have reviewed the company's financial statement and researched the company's bank balances, receivables, inventory methods, key meeting records, depreciation, and more.

While reading this brief letter, ask a lot of questions. Is the statement full of qualifiers, such as "if," "subject to," and "unless"? Does the auditor provide a "qualified" opinion on the company? If so, why does the auditor harbor doubts over the company's accounting standards?

The main point of the auditor's letter is to verify the validity of the company's financial statement and determine whether it conforms to Generally Accepted Accounting Principles. If the letter unnerves you in any way, keep this in mind while reading the rest of the report.

Many professional investors disregard this letter entirely, but a perceptibly negative report could save one some time. If the auditors have doubts, you should, too.

Profile the Prime Suspects

Letters to shareholders from the chief executive officer (CEO) and/ or president contain clues to the quality of management, the corporate culture, and the market opportunities ahead. Naturally, watch out for obfuscation: If the letter goes on for several pages but seems to say nothing at all, that's trouble. At the very least, this portion of the annual report should answer the question, "What's ahead for our company?"

Whenever possible, compare this letter with previous ones. Has the company achieved what it set out to do last year, or the year before? What can one glean from the tone of the CEO? Is this someone with whom we could chat about business, or is this someone who sounds detached and haughty? If we cannot understand the CEO, neither can the company's coworkers.

There's an old tradition in business that when things are going well, you complain, and when things are going badly, you brag. Generally speaking, we prefer managers and executives who under-promise and overdeliver—consistently. At the very least, we expect an executive's actions to align with his or her words. If the CEO's letter sounds optimistic, but filings with the SEC indicate that he or she is selling stock, this is a classic "pump and dump" scenario.

If the CEO seems to be making excuses, citing "challenges" without any clear plan for overcoming those challenges, be wary. Nearly every company that laid off workers in 2002 blamed the terrorist attacks of 2001. More than a few of these claims were unjustified.

Examine the Evidence with a Magnifying Glass

To quote songwriter Tom Waits, "The large print giveth and the small print taketh away."[3] Before you read the financial statement's information on sales, profits, inventory, and debt, read the accompanying footnotes. This is where the caveats often hide. When the financial statement's standard line items require a lot of explanatory footnotes, we turn up the sensitivity on our "nonsense" detector.

Review year-over-year figures by comparing the percentage change in each line item to the change in annual revenue. A well-managed business does everything possible to manage costs while increasing margins. However, companies that depend on innovation should not scrimp on research and development when sales are down, but should find their savings elsewhere.

Here, your overall understanding of the company helps, but so does an understanding of others in the same industry. Did market conditions affect the entire industry similarly? This gives us a point of reference for one company's performance.

Round Up the Usual Suspects

Most annual reports and proxy statements feature common elements besides those mentioned above, such as a list of directors and officers, summary of financials, and a detailed description of subsidiaries, brands, and contact information. All of these influence us. For example, we are suspicious of companies that have fewer than 5 or more than 12 directors, and we prefer a high ratio of outside, independent directors, as well as directors with a large, vested interest in the performance of the company. (Note: Heavy insider ownership does not by itself guarantee alignment of shareholders' and management interests; mismanaged incentives sometimes lead management to artificially manipulate the stock price or backdate options. Look for evidence of aligned interests in what people do, not what they say. Capital allocation, compensation standards, and other visible fiduciary duties paint a clear picture of management's attitude toward owners, including you.)

The proxy statement details insider ownership, executive salaries, stock options, bonuses, and other key details that one must weigh. For example, Johnson & Johnson's 2006 proxy statement indicates that CEO William Weldon received a $3 million bonus in 2005. Was it justified? The proxy also lays out how the bonus was determined, along with the stock's returns for shareholders, so readers can draw their own conclusions.

Accessories to the "Crime"

Krantz's *USA Today* article wisely points out that insider deals are another possible cause for concern. Look for the "related-party transactions" section of the annual report or 10-K filing to see if the company is doing business with family or friends of its own key personnel. Often, these deals are in the best interests of the shareholders, but sometimes they are not. We always question them.

Finally, the effect of changing interest rates, also highlighted in Krantz's article, must be considered. At the time of Krantz's article, interest rates had nowhere to go but up. At such times, companies that depend too much on debt pay a huge penalty, even if interest rates grow very slowly. However, companies like Automatic Data Processing, which manages outsourced payroll, could benefit significantly when rates go up, because they earn interest on the "float" while processing payroll checks.

Making the Case

Every public company is a unique entity, and no two annual reports are exactly alike. As investment detectives, we approach each new report with an open mind and earnest curiosity. We expect the annual report to help us understand how a company works and how it will prosper in the future.

But we also approach with caution and skepticism; after all, it's our money. The annual report, proxy statement, and 10-K filings are only three pieces of a very big puzzle, but they are key pieces. They are the company's case for why we should invest. If they make their case well, they earn further research. If not, there are many other companies worthy of our investment, and like U.S. Marshal Sam Gerard, we'll keep sleuthing away until we find our "man."

Annual report sleuths should learn about the company's pension plan. Any shortfalls (unfunded portions) of the pension plan or other benefits come right out of the company's cash, affecting both its stability and flexibility. But the information may be hard to interpret, as described by columnist Bill Mann, commenting on General Motors' (GM) $25 billion pension deficit:

> There are a few crazy things about this. First, due to the vagaries of Generally Accepted Accounting Practices in the U.S., this massive liability does not show up on GM's consolidated balance sheet. Further, the nearly $10 billion in losses GM's pension suffered in the last two years are reflected nowhere in the company's income statement, replaced instead by a number

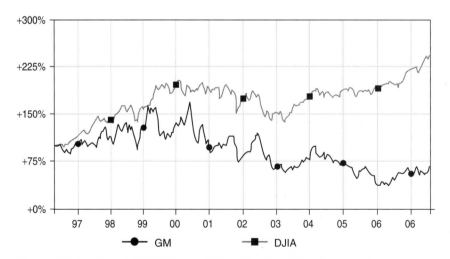

Figure 15.1   General Motors and the Pension Monster

Data Source: FT Interactive Data via Capital IQ, a division of Standard & Poor's that represented what was expected to happen based upon assumptions drawn up by GM itself. To mark the absurdity of this treatment, consider this: According to GAAP, GM got to report an expected gain on its pension in 2002 of $7.1 billion, even though its actual return on assets was a negative $4.9 billion. Big difference.

In 2003, GM addressed its pension problem, borrowing money at low rates and investing very successfully; in 2007, they moved much of their impressive gains into bonds and it appears that their pension is now secure and fully funded, but cheap loans and great market gains are not always available (see Figure 15.1). Mann points out that GM should serve as a warning to anyone planning to invest in a company with a pension plan: "The company you hold, or the one you are analyzing, may have an enormous pension liability that you cannot see on the balance sheet or income statement, but is instead buried in the footnotes." Didn't we tell you to read the footnotes first?

CHAPTER

16

How Inventory Can Skew the Financials

We sometimes refer to *inventory* as the dirtiest word in business. Certainly, inventory presents one of the great management challenges and one of the great valuation mysteries when considering a company for investment. Annual reports and financial statements cite inventory, but the number cannot always be taken at face value.

In 1992, the director of Florida International University's Center for Accounting, Auditing, and Tax Studies told the *Wall Street Journal*, "When companies are desperate to stay afloat, inventory fraud is the easiest way to produce instant profits and dress up the balance sheet." We'll cite some examples, but note that even when inventory is properly managed and properly accounted for, its true value may not be obvious to the prospective investor.

Rogue's Gallery of Fraud

A web search on "inventory fraud" turns up many references to the "Salad Oil Scandal," which was an audacious scam uncovered in 1963. Apparently, the Allied Crude Vegetable Oil Company learned that banks would make loans secured by inventory. Since oil floats on water, the company easily faked massive inventory by filling tanks with water and floating some oil on top for the benefit of inspectors. When the fraud was finally discovered, over $175 million in salad oil was missing, and that's a lot of lettuce.

Another famous inventory-related fraud involved the Crazy Eddie's appliance/hi-fi chain. Crazy Eddie's high-energy television ads were a legendary late-night staple in the northeastern United States. The conspirators in this case used nearly every possible trick to fool auditors and overvalue their inventory. They offered to help the auditors and then simply exaggerated counts in the warehouses. They got suppliers to ship merchandise but hold the invoices. They moved stock between stores so it would get counted twice. Thus, Crazy Eddie's appeared very profitable because its revenues seemed to come from selling fewer items at higher margins.

In August 2004, Bristol-Myers Squibb (BMY) settled charges stemming from the inflation of sales by $2.5 billion over a three-year period, achieved by making wholesalers buy more products than they could manage (talk about a cockroach!). A 1999 study by the Committee of Sponsoring Organizations of the Treadway Commission showed that misstated asset valuations account for nearly half of all financial statement fraud, and overvalued inventory makes up nearly all of the exaggerated asset valuations. Clearly, we must pay attention to inventory.

The Value of Inventory

Scoundrels manipulate inventory because it is easy and because it is important to the valuation of the company. Inventory represents assets, at least from an accounting point of view. But determining the value of inventory is problematic. Joseph T. Wells, founder of the Association of Certified Fraud Examiners, explains it this way:

> The valuation of inventory involves two separate elements: quantity and price. Determining the quantity of inventory on hand is often difficult. Goods are constantly being bought and sold, transferred among locations and added during a manufacturing process. Figuring the unit cost of inventory can be problematic, too; FIFO, LIFO, average cost and other valuation methods can routinely make a material difference in what the final inventory is worth.[1]

Items in stock come and go throughout the accounting period, often at diverse prices, so a standard must be applied. FIFO refers to first in, first out; whereas LIFO refers to last in, first out. Under FIFO accounting, the ending inventory is based on the cost of the most recent units brought into inventory, whereas under LIFO, the ending inventory is based on the oldest units in stock.

The Game of LIFO

Companies choose LIFO or FIFO to suit their particular type of inventory, usually related to how an item's value or cost typically changes over time. When prices are rising, FIFO gives a lower cost of goods sold (COGS) and a higher income amount than LIFO. Under the same conditions, LIFO equates to lower income and therefore lower taxation, which improves cash flow. Of course, when costs are dropping, all of this is reversed.

> The key concept to keep in mind is this:
> Gross margin (profit) equals sales minus cost of goods sold.

How a company accounts for inventory determines the COGS, and therefore the apparent profit. We may better understand the ongoing profitability of a company using LIFO, because the COGS is based on the most recent inventory, which more closely resembles today's actual costs. But in the case of appreciating inventory, such as antiques, LIFO may understate inventory value. An entrepreneurial investor applies his or her knowledge of inventory management to develop insights about the financial realities of an inventory-intensive company.

When a company changes from one method to the other, such as Chrysler did in the 1970s, they may be trying to manipulate value, and we are highly suspicious of such drastic changes. Sometimes the change in inventory accounting methods is announced by nothing more than a footnote in the annual report. Companies sometimes make such moves to avoid violation of debt covenants or to make earnings appear stronger than they really are. Prospective investors must read between the lines of financial statements to better understand the impact of inventory accounting.

The Inventory Management Tightrope

In addition to how inventory is counted and valued, we must understand its role in the day-to-day business. Generally, we don't like inventory because it costs money to buy and costs money to store, but some companies must maintain high levels. In fact, some make inventory their competitive advantage. Hardware giant Home Depot

(HD) has to maintain a massive inventory because if it runs out of hammers, people can get them (and everything else) at Lowe's (LOW).

Technology companies, however, need to keep inventory levels as low as possible, or they risk getting stuck with obsolete products. Many software companies have become service companies and carry *no* inventory, delivering all products and updates online. Computer hardware keeps improving, but the prices continue to drop. Manufacturers face the risk of obsolescence nearly as soon as a product is released.

Some manufacturers constrain supply to keep their margins high and their inventory low, but end up walking a dangerous tightrope. Two notable examples are Harley-Davidson (HOG) motorcycles and Nikon cameras. Harley has long used inventory management to keep prices high; it worries little about obsolescence because nostalgia is central to its value proposition. People buy Harleys because the technology and styling is dated. Nikon, however, had to change its approach with the advent of digital photography. In the days of film, Nikon could introduce a new camera, knowing that the model would be in its lineup for many years. Today, Nikon introduces new digital cameras every few months; any excess inventory represents potential losses, so, like Harley-Davidson, it constrains supply. Unfortunately, this has resulted in long wait times, frustrated prospective customers, and lost sales for both companies. Inventory management is more than an accounting issue; it is also a strategic marketing challenge.

Seasonality also affects the value of inventory. A large supply of lawn care products in the Northeast becomes a lot less valuable as winter approaches. Home Depot can transfer lawn care products to its stores in the Southwest as snow falls in the Northeast, but toy stores walk a considerably higher tightrope. On December 20, a high inventory level is very valuable. On December 26, leftover inventory might become worthless and lead to write-downs (unless we're talking about an antique toy store, since inventory could appreciate over time).

Adding Value, Not Revenue

Understanding the role of inventory includes the recognition that some inventory adds value without directly adding revenue. Many service-oriented companies offer amenities that enhance customer experience but are not sold. This could include gift-wrapping in a toy store, or use of office supplies in a copy shop. Dogmatic bean counters often miss the added value of such amenities and their effect on customer loyalty. We've seen executives lobby for the removal of such conveniences, even though it would be like removing salt and pepper from restaurants because condiments are not a profit center.

Obsession with margin can lead to misunderstood inventory. For example, a photo lab (service) that also sells frames (merchandise) probably earns a much higher profit margin on the service. In such situations, misguided managers may actually discourage merchandise sales so the overall profit percentage will look better, even if the actual profit dollars are lowered. We find such strategies perplexing because, as we often say, "you don't take percentages to the bank."

Taking Care of Turnover

Elvis Presley wore a diamond-encrusted ring that said "TCB," for "taking care of business." An acquaintance of ours who managed a Kmart store in the 1970s wore a gold ring that said "TO," for "turnover." "Turnover was our mantra in those days," he explains. "We bought merchandise on a 90-day net arrangement and tried to turn the entire store every 2 weeks."

In other words, when all was going well, Kmart would sell every item in the store and earn profit six times before it paid for the first batch of inventory. Clearly, there's more to great management than turnover, but anyone saddled with an inventory-intensive business better be obsessed with turning that merchandise.

Some inventory is very liquid and therefore less risky. Inventory that turns reliably and quickly, like that of Coca-Cola, Wrigley, and Hershey (HSY), is probably as good as cash, and as you surely know by now, we think pretty highly of cash when researching prospective investments.

Solving the Inventory Mystery

Sir Arthur Conan Doyle's Sherlock Holmes noted that false modesty is no less a lie than bragging. Likewise, overvalued inventory is not the only mystery to be investigated by prospective investors. Hidden assets may also lurk in inventory; consider the antique toy store reference earlier. Trendy toys are a liability after the holiday season, but antique toys usually do not lose value. Any product or commodity that appreciates over time could easily—and honestly—be undervalued in a financial statement.

However, "ending inventory" usually represents merchandise or material that simply didn't sell well, or at least hasn't sold yet. In the fashion industry, the best styles sell quickly and the rest hang in the store, losing value every day. The same logic applies to computer chips, cars, and furniture.

Investors need to look far beyond the quantity and reported value of items in inventory. To understand the real meaning of this and other assets, one must understand the methods of valuation, the nature of the products in inventory, and the external market factors

Jake's Toy Store   BALANCE SHEET
Palm Springs, California
December 31, 2001

Cash	$100,000	Accounts Payable	$250,000
Inventory (*Note 1*)	$200,000		
Current Assets	$300,000	Current Liabilities	$250,000
Land & Building (*Note 2*)	$100,000	Mortgage on Property (*Note 2*)	$200,000
Total Assets	$400,000	Total Liabilities	$450,000
		Equity	($50,000)
			$400,000

Jake's Toy Store Income Statement
January 1 - December 31,2001

Sales	$1,000,000
Cost of Sales	$500,000
Operating Costs	$300,000
Net Income	$200,000

1. What is the current ratio?
2. What is the inventory turn?
3. What is the debt-to-equity ratio?
4. What is the break-even point?
5. What do you think are the problems and opportunities for the owner?

Note 1: LIFO Method (Last In First Out)
Note 2: Land and Building Purchased in 1949 - Refinanced in 1981

Figure 16.1   Jake's Toy Store, Part 2

that might affect value in the real world, which may or may not bear any resemblance to the financial statement.

Have you been thinking about Jake's Toy Store since the end of Chapter 14? We may as well tell you now: It was a trick exercise. The questions in the figure are easily answered and almost completely pointless, because there is too much they do not tell us about Jake's. Let's read between the lines (see Figure 16.1).

Inventory is listed as an asset, but it's after Christmas and the store uses the LIFO inventory system. In other words, the store's current inventory is old merchandise. Does this mean the inventory is worthless? Not necessarily. If Jake's is an antique toy store, the inventory could be appreciating as time passes.

However, Jake's Toy Store might have nothing to do with toys. Jake might be a real estate baron. The building and land were bought in 1949, so Jake might be enjoying over 50 years' worth of appreciation in one of the most exclusive real estate markets in the world. Moreover, Jake may have picked up a lot of Palm Springs real estate in the 1950s, when barren desert was available for a fraction of today's prices.

The best way to know for sure is to visit the store. If one cannot visit, compare this statement to previous statements for a better understanding of the cash and sales. The moral of the story? Treat a financial statement as a source of questions, not answers.

CHAPTER 17

Great First Impressions: 10 Signs of a Strong Company

Warren Buffett once explained that "price is what you pay, value is what you get." Naturally, an entrepreneurial investor seeks companies that offer a lot of value for a low price, but prices fluctuate. Thus, price helps determine *when* to buy, but a host of other factors influence *what* to buy. We look for 10 specific strengths when evaluating a company. This is not the same concept as "valuation," which estimates the financial value of a company and is the topic of Part Four. Rather, here we're talking about the factors that suggest a company of quality and cause us to fire up our valuation assessments. Few companies master all 10 areas, but the following areas comprise the first set of hurdles a company must face before they get our full attention.

1. A Simple Business Model

The very first issue of our *Exclusive Outlook* newsletter sang the praises of simple companies. We refuse to invest in something we do not understand, and observe that over the years Wall Street has also tended to reward simple, focused companies. Simple companies are easy to understand for customers, coworkers, management, and investors, easing alignment of interests. When considering a company, expect to quickly understand how it makes money, and how it makes money for *you*. In that first issue of *Exclusive Outlook*, we could not explain what JDS Uniphase sells, and we still cannot. Wal-Mart, on the other hand, makes instant sense to us. Wal-Mart offers everyday goods at steep discounts and manages its supply chain to maintain profits.

2. A "Wide-Moat" Competitive Advantage

Competitive advantage comes in many forms, as we discussed in Chapter 8, but usually comes from a cost management edge or market differentiation. Just as in a medieval castle, the wider the moat, the greater the barrier to entry. We prefer unassailable companies because, by definition, they possess a long-term profit advantage and gain both pricing and buying power. Although competitive advantage may be less tangible than real estate or cash in the bank, it is nevertheless an essential element in a stock's margin of safety. Although we've been reading for years about companies that hope to topple Microsoft, the company's nearly complete market share keeps competitors at a safe distance. Cisco Systems, however, lacks the market dominance, cost advantage, or unique positioning to keep competitors at bay.

3. Recurring Revenue

As we often say, cash flow is the lifeblood of business, and a company with any form of annuity revenue streams is more attractive than a company without them. These may appear in the form of long-term contracts for services, or in the form of ubiquitous products used every day, such as chewing gum, shaving razors, or soft drinks. Lamar Advertising's billboards produce advance bookings and long-term monthly revenues from repeat clients, whereas Toll Brothers homebuilding business depends on large, one-time purchases.

4. Low Inventory Risk

Any product that can go out of style or become obsolete presents inventory risk. Even a costly item that sells slowly results in additional opportunity costs for whoever holds the inventory. Dell Computer's early success came from managing the inventory risk caused by the rapid evolution of personal computers. By building to order from "just in time" parts, Dell minimized what had been a costly challenge for PC makers. Not all types of inventory are bad, of course. Retailers like Lowe's and The Home Depot need massive inventories as part of their market strategy, but a fashion retailer like The Gap has to discount inventory virtually every season as styles change. We prefer companies with highly liquid inventory that turns quickly and reliably, such as Hershey's chocolates or Coca-Cola.

5. Alignment of Interests

Look for evidence of aligned interests in what people do, not what they say. Capital allocation, compensation standards, and other visible fiduciary duties paint a clear picture of management's attitude toward owners, including you. We like high levels of insider ownership, but that does not tell the whole story. Devotion to per-share value and long-term strategic planning, including succession planning, are more important. Consider the case of National Home Health Care, where high inside ownership did not equate to alignment of interests, because the entrenched management sought to sell the company at a price other shareholders considered too low, but in a deal that ensured many benefits for themselves. However, recall the example of ATP Oil and Gas, which designed incentive programs that rewarded coworkers with new cars for benefiting shareholders, aligning interests at every level of the organization.

6. A Healthy Culture

As Jim Collins observed in *Good to Great* (HarperCollins, 2001), the best leaders tend to be workhorses, not show horses. They have great ambition, but for the company rather than for themselves. This helps a company withstand change and builds zealousness in coworkers. Ruthless cultures tend to attract or produce workers more interested in managing their careers than the business. Adelphia faced allegation after allegation of ethics violations and questionable business practices, and its leaders have recently been sent to jail. Contrast the morale of Adelphia employees with that of Johnson & Johnson coworkers, whose company credo makes them feel part of a visionary, honest, ethical, and loyal team.

7. A Flat Organizational Structure

Frankly, nothing complicates a business quite as much as people, especially management. Look for companies that get the job done with as few people as possible, in as few layers as possible. A quick "cocktail napkin" comparison of revenue or market capitalization per coworker tells us much about the labor efficiency of companies in the same industry. High revenues per coworker suggest truly engaged and frugal management. Of course, one mustn't trade effectiveness for efficiency, so labor costs cannot be considered out of context. For example, it makes sense for a company with ambitious growth plans to be "overstaffed" in anticipation of future workloads. The Tribune Company, and most other newspaper publishers, historically depended on high head counts to cover local, national, and international news, but that business model no longer works, and many daily newspapers laid off workers or announced layoffs over the past three years. Can these businesses survive without the human talent that defined them? On the other extreme, oil and gas exploration company Contango, with a market cap of almost $600 million, manages its entire operation with a staff of only six people.

8. Low Reinvention Risk

Why go looking for trouble? We love Apple's products and are huge fans of Steve Jobs, but our stomachs cannot bear the thought of investing in the company, which must continuously innovate, and must hit a towering home run (iMac, iPod, iPhone?) every two or three years—without fail! Conversely, we often joke about the Wrigley annual meeting, where we imagine a tough decision every year is whether to change the color of the chewing gum wrapper.

9. Low Capital Requirements

As Groucho Marx might have said, "All else being equal, math class wouldn't be so hard." Well, all else being equal, we like companies with lots of cash, but we don't like companies that *need* lots of cash. Very high capital requirements did not kill manufacturing and the automobile industry in this country, but they sure helped. Many of us don't understand why Detroit resists new fuel economy standards when it seems so simple to make fuel-efficient cars, but such changes are not as easy as they may seem. Redesigning and retooling would cost Detroit a fortune, and even though it's the correct long-term strategy, no one likes to spend that kind of money. Generally, high capital requirements make companies less agile and, ultimately, less competitive. Google, on the other hand, needs comparatively little capital (considering its humongous market capitalization) to try a lot of new ideas and execute the best.

10. Favorable Demographics

The world is constantly changing, and while the most dramatic changes cannot be predicted, many trends can be recognized and acted on. Which companies might benefit from the growing wealth of the so-called BRIC (Brazil, Russia, India, and China) nations? Which companies might thrive if inflation soars? Whether from far-sightedness or plain old good luck, some companies are better positioned for predicted shifts in world demographics. For example, wealthier countries' populations are aging, which bodes well for diversified health care companies like Johnson & Johnson. However, music companies like EMI seemed completely unprepared and were slow to respond to advances in technology and the changing demands of young consumers. As more musicians publish and distribute their own works over the Internet, what role might a record company play?

A company that looks good in these 10 areas would seem a strong company indeed. But certain factors weigh more heavily in certain situations, so we cannot consider any of these attributes in a vacuum. When is simplicity more important than recurring revenue? When is alignment of interests more important than inventory risk? Each company must be measured in context, considering its industry, regulatory environment, demographics, price, and other factors.

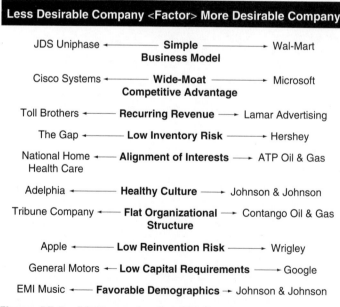

Figure 17.1   10 Signs of a Quality Company

Checklists and formulae may help to order our thinking, but choosing companies worth owning still requires artful judgment.

The companies in Figure 17.1 illustrate the range of possibilities when considering the 10 criteria. Any single company that leans to the "more desirable" side on most of these factors is a strong contender for our attention.

CHAPTER 18

Inspirational Figures:
Bernard Baruch[1]

Disciplined Opportunist, Pragmatic Idealist

"Never pay the slightest attention to what a company president ever says about his stock." So said Bernard Mannes Baruch, one of the greatest investors in history. A man of uncommon common sense, Baruch understood that even the best-intentioned company president lacks objectivity. After all, not many racehorse owners would tell you, "I think my horse is going to lose today!"

Baruch's plainspoken common sense contrasts sharply with his legendary status on Wall Street. People expect magical pronouncements, but when asked what the stock market would do in the future, Baruch replied, "It will fluctuate."

Baruch's vanity and his publicists' skill overbuilt his reputation; his success seemed to result from magical powers, and there's nothing to be learned from someone who succeeds through unnatural talent. However, biographer James Grant, seeking to puncture the myths surrounding Baruch, came away even more impressed: ". . . the success that the mortal Baruch enjoyed through trial and error was harder won than any that the legendary Baruch might have achieved through pure clairvoyance."

Fickle Fame, Enduring Wisdom

Despite his reputation as one of the most powerful men of the early twentieth century, most people under 60 only recognize the name

Bernard Baruch as a frequent source of quotations in financial or political literature.

Born in 1870 and living to the ripe old age of 94, Baruch's lifetime spanned the Industrial Revolution; two world wars; the stock market crash and Depression; and the assassinations of Presidents Garfield, McKinley, and Kennedy.

An astute self-promoter, Baruch garnered much of his fame as an economic adviser to politicians and presidents for over 40 years, from Wilson to Kennedy. He garnered his fortune as a dispassionate speculator in the stock market. Highly controversial in both endeavors, Baruch stands as an icon of individualism, intelligence, and perhaps above all, the discipline to see facts clearly, and to act on those facts rather than on his feelings.

Success leaves clues, and Bernard Baruch was an extremely successful investor. His life story and many of his most famous quotations describe an investment philosophy with lessons for all of us.

"Never Follow the Crowd"

Born in South Carolina, where his father had emigrated from Germany in 1855, Baruch moved with his family to New York City in 1881. In 1889, nineteen-year-old Bernard graduated from college and soon took his first job as an "office boy," earning $3 a week. In 1891, he took a similar job on Wall Street, but quickly rose through the ranks.

As a broker and later a partner at A. Housman and Company, Baruch saved his money and bought his own seat on the New York Stock Exchange in 1897. Over the next few years he made a fortune, usually through outright speculation and shorting of stocks (*shorting* refers to selling a stock one does not yet own, with the belief that the share price will go down and the stock can be purchased back for less than its original selling price).

An example of Baruch's pragmatic approach to the market came with the assassination of President McKinley. According to one story, while other high profile financiers like J. P. Morgan mused to reporters that the assassination might be bad for the stock market, Baruch acted, shorting copper stocks and quickly earning the equivalent of $15 million in today's dollars. While others worried, Baruch acted on the facts before him.

Short-sellers are not well loved in the investment world, because their positions can create additional volatility, and because, as in the example above, they seem cold-bloodedly opportunistic. But Baruch's job was to make money for his clients (and himself), so he was bullish (expecting the market to rise) or bearish (expecting the market to fall) as he felt the facts dictated.

In 1903, Baruch launched his own brokerage house, and by 1910 his reputation as a Wall Street powerhouse was secure. Although known for his fierce independence, he owed much of his success to the relationships he built among the most influential people of the day. At one time or another, Baruch partnered with nearly all the famous names of early Wall Street, including the Guggenheim family, J. P. Morgan, and railroad magnate Edward H. Harriman. Baruch was bright, friendly, handsome, and active; people enjoyed his company, and he made friends easily. Friends offered inside information and he profited from it (there was no Securities and Exchange Commission at the time—what we now call "insider information" was then considered research; it was also notoriously unreliable).

He tried many types of investments, but specialized in mining. According to biographer James Grant, "It was Baruch's settled opinion that nobody could know all investments thoroughly and that it was best to stick to what one knew best." This is what contemporary investing legend Warren Buffett refers to as *circle of competence.*

Famous for his intelligence, wealth, and connections, Baruch chaired the War Industries Board during World War I, advised Franklin D. Roosevelt on the economics of the "New Deal," declined the office of Treasury Secretary during World War II, and served on the United Nations Atomic Energy Commission for President Truman. He appeared on the cover of *Time* magazine in 1924, 1928, and 1943. For nearly his entire adult life, presidents, senators, bankers, and investors sought Baruch's advice.

A lifelong idealist, Baruch became close friends with President Woodrow Wilson and a supporter of his League of Nations initiative. Baruch joined Wilson's team at the Versailles peace conference, and lobbied hard for less draconian economic punishments for the German people. He lost this battle, and by nearly all accounts, the seeds for World War II were sown. For the rest of his life, Baruch spent much of his political capital looking for ways to "take the profit out of war." He believed that wars would happen less often and end sooner if the flames were not fanned by profiteers. Unfortunately, this idea still has not caught on.

Late in life, he was called the "Park Bench Statesman," because he was known to do his best thinking in Washington, D.C.'s, Lafayette Park and in New York City's Central Park. Some claimed his office was a park bench near the White House.

Baruch's listeners didn't always agree with his point of view, but all except the most extreme seemed to appreciate his candor (fringe groups have branded Baruch's recommendations for international control of nuclear technology and weapons as a Zionist plot for world domination).

Although his political adventures occupied most of his long life, we are grateful for the lessons of his Wall Street years. Following are some quotations from Bernard Baruch, and our comments on the meaning for investors of today.

On "The Facts"

- If you get all the facts, your judgment can be right; if you don't get all the facts, it can't be right.
- Approach each new problem not with a view of finding what you hope will be there, but to get the truth, the realities that must be grappled with. You may not like what you find. In that case you are entitled to try to change it. But do not deceive yourself as to what you do find to be the facts of the situation.
- Every man has a right to his opinion, but no man has a right to be wrong in his facts.
- Know your own failings, passions, and prejudices so you can separate them from what you see.

Although he left the detailed work of deal making to trusted lawyers and more capable friends, Baruch believed in hands-on research. He traveled all over the world to meet personally with mine owners, smelter operators, and others who had firsthand knowledge of companies in which he might invest. He wanted to see operations for himself, and he wanted to look the people in the eye.

More importantly, he worked to see the facts clearly and not be swayed by emotion or opinion. Most people lack the discipline to do this, but as we said before, his job was to make money, and acting on facts rather than feelings helped him do so. His comment about separating one's prejudices and passions from that which you see echoes our own frequent comment: Your eyes believe what they see; your ears believe others.

On Discipline

- The greatest blessing of our democracy is freedom. But in the last analysis, our only freedom is the freedom to discipline ourselves.
- Two things are bad for the heart—running up stairs and running down people.

An omnipresent theme in Baruch's philosophy was that discipline is the foundation for a well-ordered life and good decisions. For investors, the discipline to be ruled by one's intelligence is the discipline to separate facts from feelings, and the discipline to maintain relationships through thick and thin. Baruch was not perfect on either front, but worked at both. As a result, his triumphs were not always as great as some thought they should have been, but his failures were also less costly. Ultimately, he sought the discipline to follow his own advice; he was quite comfortable in his own skin, as the saying goes.

On the Stock Market

- Don't try to buy at the bottom and sell at the top. It can't be done except by liars.
- I made my money by selling too soon.
- I never lost money by turning a profit.
- If a speculator is correct half of the time, he is hitting a good average. Even being right 3 or 4 times out of 10 should yield a person a fortune if he has the sense to cut his losses quickly on the ventures where he is wrong.
- The main purpose of the stock market is to make fools of as many men as possible.
- When good news about the market hits the front page of the *New York Times*, sell.

These six statements present a gold mine of good advice for investors; they sound familiar because they are so often quoted or paraphrased by investing greats such as Warren Buffett and

Peter Lynch. Our favorite, which captures Baruch's wry sense of humor, is the sentiment that he never lost money by turning a profit. Like the first two quotations, Baruch here makes the point that the goal of investing is not the achievement of some academic perfection, but the accumulation of capital.

Too many amateur investors worry about what they have missed rather than setting specific goals and showing the discipline to act on them. Baruch took profits that were acceptable to him. Some people chided him when the stocks continued to rise, but no one laughed at the fact that Baruch escaped three major Wall Street panics (including the crash of 1929) with his fortune intact. He preferred the consequences of getting out too soon to the consequences of staying in too late.

There's an old saying on Wall Street that the bulls can win, and the bears can win, but the pigs get slaughtered. Bernard Baruch was sometimes a bull and sometimes a bear, but never a pig. He was a disciplined opportunist who did his homework, took chances, appreciated his successes, and learned from his mistakes.

PART IV

WHAT'S IT WORTH—TO *ME?*

If we seem mildly perturbed when asked if we practice "value" or "growth" investing, it is only that we question the question. Shouldn't every investment be a good value? Don't we want all of our investments to grow, and doesn't growth increase value? Mass marketing of investment products over the last 30 years has obscured and over-complicated some of the basic concepts that drive good investing habits. Earlier sections offered ideas for understanding a business and its finances; this section offers some simple rules of thumb for evaluating the risks and rewards of investment choices.

- The ABCs of inefficiency offer a shorthand description of a good value.
- The price you pay is the key determinant of returns.
- Use the present value of future cash flows to compare investment opportunities.
- Take the long view. Most people don't.
- Intrinsic value is a mosaic of four essential pieces.
- Epilogue: The Fortune Cookie that Ate Wall Street.

CHAPTER 19

The ABCs of Market Inefficiency

The efficient market theory (EMT) claims that it is impossible for an investor to outperform the stock market because existing share prices already incorporate and reflect all relevant information and expectations. Burton Malkiel, an economics professor at Princeton University, helped lay the foundations for EMT in his book *A Random Walk Down Wall Street* (W. W. Norton & Company, 1973). In it, he writes, ". . . a blindfolded monkey throwing darts at a newspaper's financial pages could select a portfolio that would do just as well as one carefully selected by the experts."[1]

We disagree, for the most part. We believe the market tries to be efficient—and, in fact, constantly moves toward efficiency—but frequent inefficiencies produce outstanding opportunities for investors. As for the blindfolded monkey, we do not doubt he could match the investment performance of many "experts," but it really depends on how you define the term *expert*. Malkiel defends his theory by showing that during the past 30 years more than two thirds of professional portfolio managers have been outperformed by the unmanaged Standard & Poor's (S&P) 500 Index, and managers who beat the index in one period are unlikely to do so in the next.

This certainly seems like compelling evidence for EMT, considering that most investment managers are well educated and experienced. However, we believe that when taken in its proper context, the statistic can not only be explained, but provides support for our theory that the stock market is inefficient.

The False Safety of the Crowd

Established investment managers and financial institutions have little to gain by outperforming the stock market and everything to lose by underperforming. The overall stock market has returned approximately 10 percent per year over time, and an average investor would be happy with this result. Delivering 12 percent per year is no small task, but would earn analysts and money managers little more than a nice pat on the back, while 6 percent would likely get them fired.

As a result, the majority of investment managers seek a safe middle ground by owning a widely diversified group of popular stocks such as Intel and General Electric. The end result is a portfolio highly correlated to the broad stock market or its benchmark index, delivering average market returns. After fees are deducted, it is no surprise that more than two thirds of investment managers underperform. That a large number of overprotective "experts" settle for mediocre results does not mean the market itself is efficient. In many ways, their actions help make the market less efficient because herd activity distorts prices by disconnecting them from a company's true value. This is the opposite of efficiency.

Taking the prudent practice of diversification to counterproductive extremes, professionals illustrate the concept known as *diffusion of responsibility*. This social psychological phenomenon has been studied since 1964, when at least 38 people witnessed the murder of Kitty Genovese in New York City, and not a single person helped her or even called the police. Diffusion of responsibility is broadly defined as a situation in which individuals in a group assume less personal responsibility for negative consequences of a poor decision as the group becomes larger. On Wall Street, diffusion of responsibility might sound something like this: "We all took a hit" or "No one saw this coming."

Large public companies often have as many as 10 or 20 analysts covering them, and guess what happens when one of these companies misses a step? Diffusion of responsibility kicks in: No analyst wants to be the last to downgrade a stock, and no one wants to be left holding the bag when the last investor moves on to greener pastures. Wall Street is often described as a huge cocktail party where the last person remaining has to clean up: Everyone has a lovely time, but everyone also watches the door, and when someone makes a move, there is a mad rush to leave.

This vicious cycle of cheerful celebration and panicked retreat often results in capitulation of a company's stock price, and may create opportunity for more rational observers. Thanks to modern technology, trading capabilities are now available to millions of emotional investors with itchy fingers, multiplying the market's capacity for volatility and inefficiency. While the huge buying power of institutional investors mitigates the effect of individual investors' impulsive trades, even the institutions are managed by people, and the human element ensures a steady supply of inefficiency—and opportunity.

Fitting Evidence to the EMT Conclusion

It is not uncommon for zealots to use selective data to support a predetermined conclusion, to the point where they refuse to acknowledge evidence that contradicts their belief. As one story goes, a finance professor and a student come upon a $100 bill lying on the ground. The student stoops to pick it up. "Don't bother," says the professor, "If it were really a $100 bill, the efficient market theory says it wouldn't be there."

EMT proponents believe the market cannot be beaten over time, and they gather evidence that supports their belief. Such evidence is easily found in the "experts" who cannot reliably beat the market. Proponents conveniently ignore the consistently successful investors, partially because they are hard to see in the first place (many of the world's best investors manage their money privately) and partially because they invalidate the EMT.

Taking Advantage of Market Inefficiencies

There are thousands of publicly traded companies for investors to choose from, each an entirely different organism with a unique capital structure and its own problems and opportunities. At any given time, each company may be underpriced, fairly priced, or overpriced relative to an investor's alternative opportunities such as real estate, bonds, or other stocks.

EMT claims that the stock market cannot be beaten, except through insider trading or incredible luck. Forgive our trite retort, but as the old saying goes, "The man who says it cannot be done is often interrupted by the man who is doing it."

The ABCs of Investing

To take advantage of market inefficiencies, every investor wants to buy low and sell high. We think buying low is the really tricky part. An astute investor must discover value that others have not yet noticed or do not fully understand or appreciate. To improve one's odds of success, remember the ABCs of investing: Assets, Bargain, and Catalyst. In other words, seek companies that boast real, measurable assets, which can be acquired at a bargain price, the value of which may be increased by a catalytic event, such as a merger or new business development.

Try to Buy Companies for Free

Recall our obsession with "margin of safety." In ABC terms, if one can buy assets at a deep enough discount, one can profit even if a catalyst does not materialize. In other words, as the market moves toward efficiency and stock prices come to reflect a company's true value, one realizes a reasonable return. When the catalyst does occur, the gains may be outsized.

Consider the case of Saucony shoes. In mid-2003, Saucony had a market capitalization of $88 million, with net working capital of $70 million and a beautiful headquarters building worth $10 million. After netting out these assets, the entire company was selling for $8 million (because one owns the assets when one buys the company). At the time, Saucony was generating approximately $133 million in annual sales, $7.3 million in earnings, and $13 million in free cash flow. And one could buy all this—in effect—for $8 million!

So, clearly, Saucony's assets were available at a bargain price. Converse had recently been purchased by Nike (NKE) for one-and-a-half times sales plus the assumption of debt. That formula would equate to at least $200 million for Saucony, not including its $80 million in tangible assets. During early 2004, Saucony rewarded shareholders with a special cash dividend of $26 million ($4 per share). That was nice enough, but the true catalyst came when Saucony was acquired at a premium price by Stride Rite (SRR) in mid-2005.

After the Great Depression, when Benjamin Graham was formulating the tenets of value investing, people were so wary of the stock market that one could regularly find companies selling for less than the value of their net tangible assets. From an entrepreneurial investor's point of view, that would be like buying the company for free. The case of Saucony—$80 million worth of concrete assets for $88 million—comes close enough to illustrate the point nicely.

Easy as ABC?

Buy low and sell high. Investing is just that simple—and just that difficult. Finding undervalued companies is our business and our passion; online research capabilities improve our ability to generate ideas and refine our process. The real challenge for most people is discipline, the commitment to follow their ABCs. Even so, that commitment will only improve one's odds; it does not guarantee success. Consider Lone Star Steakhouse.

In January 2004, Lone Star had tons of net cash and real estate on its balance sheet, generated plentiful free cash flow, and paid healthy dividends. In addition, it had high insider ownership, was aggressively repurchasing stock, and had just authorized an additional repurchase up to 10 percent of the shares outstanding.

Nevertheless, the company featured a low market capitalization because Wall Street did not like the volatility of beef prices due to mad cow disease and the Atkins diet—one a scare and the other a fad. So the company's assets were available for a bargain price; in fact, there was very little downside. Potential catalysts at the time included the possibility of a buyout (which had been unsuccessfully attempted a few years prior) or a large special cash dividend or share repurchase funded by the monetization of the company's real estate assets. An entrepreneurial investor would have found this situation quite tempting.

But in late 2005, the company decided to stop repurchasing stock and instead reinvest in its existing restaurants in an effort to boost same-store sales. In addition, the company experienced a steep increase in operating costs due primarily to higher wages and rising commodity prices. At this point, the scenario had changed enough that our hypothetical investor would have sold and taken the loss, because the company no longer fit an entrepreneurial strategy. Fortunately, the margin of safety achieved by buying the assets at a bargain price would minimize the loss.

The ABCs are a good guide for prudent investing. Look for assets of undeniable value, such as real estate, cash, patents, or oil in the ground, available at a discount price. A probable catalyst ices the cake, turning a good investment (assets purchased at a bargain)

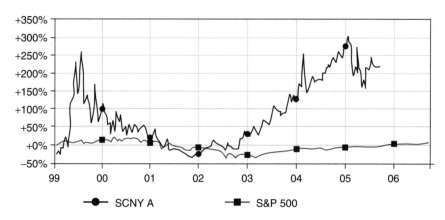

Figure 19.1   The ABCs of Opportunity

Data Source: FT Interactive Data via Capital IQ, a division of Standard & Poor's.

into a great investment (e.g., the company is acquired at a premium price).

All three components rarely coincide. When they do, profitable investing is as easy as ABC.

Saucony (SCNYA) was a good example of the opportunity to purchase assets at a bargain price, with conditions in the athletic shoe industry suggesting the probability of a catalyst in the future. (See Figure 19.1.) Such opportunities are rare; even when one can find assets at a bargain price, the catalyst does not always happen, or does not always happen in a timely manner.

But with adequate margins of safety and an opportunistic attention to detail, an entrepreneurial investor doesn't have to win them all. As Wall Street legend Bernard Baruch said, "Even being right 3 or 4 times out of 10 should yield a person a fortune if he has the sense to cut his losses quickly on the ventures where he is wrong."[2] Or as we like to say, "It's okay to be wrong, but it's not okay to stay wrong."

CHAPTER 20

"Wait Till the Moon Is Full"

In Margaret Wise Brown's children's book *Wait Till the Moon Is Full* (Harper & Row, 1948), a young raccoon beseeches his mother to let him outside to see the night. But night after night, she tells him, "Wait till the moon is full."

The little raccoon waits, and when at last the moon is full, he emerges from his home to find new friends waiting and all his questions answered (including how dark is the dark, and whether or not the moon is a rabbit). His wise mother teaches the value of patience, helping him wait until a nocturnal foray will be safe, fun, and beneficial.

Naturally, this reminds us of stock picking.

When the Time Is Right

We've often written that once we conclude our research and determine that a company meets certain criteria, we add it to our watch list so we can buy it "when the time is right." To a large degree, that means "when the price is right."

Our approach depends not just on the identification of excellent companies, but also on the opportunity to purchase stock at a discount to the intrinsic value of the company. This broadens our margin of safety and improves the likelihood of stock appreciation.

How Much Did Disney Really Pay for Pixar?

The actual cost of an investment is widely misunderstood because too many people just look at the stock price. Disney CEO Robert Iger put this in perspective during an interview about Disney's acquisition of Pixar. He corrected the reporter's statement that Disney paid $7.4 billion for Pixar. "They had $1 billion in cash, so it nets down to $6.4 billion." This is an important distinction: When you buy a company, you get all of its assets, including its cash. In the case of Pixar, this reduced the apparent price by 14 percent.

Jeremy Siegel wrote about the importance of price in his Yahoo! finance column of February 23, 2006. He described the "growth trap" that snares many investors: Fast-growing stocks look like a way to make big gains, but they are often overpriced because so many people are eagerly investing in them. Siegel compared the 1950–2005 results of IBM (a fast-growing new company) and Standard Oil (a boring old company).

People turned up their noses at Standard and rushed to buy IBM. In the long run, Standard's annualized returns were about 1 percent higher than IBM's, according to Siegel. "Although this difference looks small, $1,000 invested in the oil giant in 1950 would be worth over $1.8 million today, while $1,000 invested in IBM would be worth $867,000, less than one half the amount in Standard Oil."[1]

Why? Siegel explains, "IBM lost on the valuation criterion, and valuation, the price you pay for the earnings and dividends you receive, is the primary determinant of long-term investor returns."

Criteria for Selection: Ask the Right Questions

Price and downside protection are important criteria in our selection process, as are probable catalysts and upside potential. We also prefer businesses with annuity revenue streams, low or very liquid inventory, and only as many coworkers as are needed to get the job done (sometimes reflected in revenue/coworker statistics). Naturally, we also watch the business cycle to consider how macroeconomic trends might impact different kinds of businesses. Overall, we break our search into three general categories (see Figure 20.1).

No company is perfect; indeed, weighing these factors makes up the "art" of investing. The criteria defining the business and the people are fairly stable, but the criteria related to price are more volatile and result in price inefficiencies from time to time. If your research indicates that a company is worth $40 per share and it is trading at $40 per share, wait till the moon is full. When an event that does not degrade the intrinsic value of the company degrades

The Business

Is it understandable?
Does it have competitive advantage?
Does it have recurring revenues?
How well does it manage the product life cycle?
How will demographic shifts affect this company?

The People

Are they shareholder-oriented?
Have they demonstrated competence in allocating capital?
Do they understand and manage the company culture?
Is there a high level of insider ownership?
Are they skilled operators of their business?

The Price

How does potential reward compare to risks?
What is the margin of safety?
How big is the discount to intrinsic value?
What is the current liquidation value?
How does it compare to others in the industry?

Figure 20.1 Ask the Right Questions

Data Source: FT Interactive Data via Capital IQ, a division of Standard & Poor's.

the price of the stock, perhaps driving it down to $30 per share, the moon is as big and round as a young raccoon's eyes and the time is right.

Good companies sometimes go on sale. In the spring of 2006, Microsoft (MSFT) indicated that it planned to spend quite a bit on new projects, and Wall Street hammered the stock, knocking it down about 10 percent in one day (see Figure 20.2). In the spring of 2001, Johnson & Johnson (JNJ) acquired Alza. Even though most observers declared this a good acquisition, Wall Street ritualistically punished the stock (see Figure 20.3). The fundamentals of these well-run companies did not change in a meaningful way, but the stock price dropped considerably. Imagine the opportunity for someone who bought Microsoft in June 2006 ($21.43 on June 13); by January 2007 ($31.21 on January 12) that investor would have experienced a 45 percent increase in the price.

Entrepreneurial investors maintain a watch list of excellent companies, waiting patiently for a good sale. Patience is a virtue, indeed!

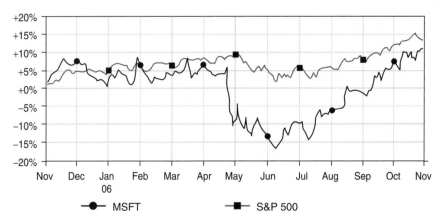

Figure 20.2   When the Price Is Right

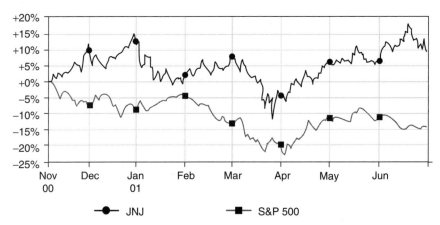

Figure 20.3   When the Price is Right, continued

Data Source: FT Interactive Data via Capital IQ, a division of Standard & Poor's.

21

Today's Price for Tomorrow's Growth: The X Factor

Wall Street analysts earn big bucks for taking on a very difficult task: estimating the value of public companies. How helpful are these highly paid experts? Well, in June 2006, 22 analysts were following Johnson & Johnson. Their one-year price targets ranged from $56.40 to $76.00, so they firmly believed that JNJ stock would go either up or down, possibly quite a bit. As such, their recommendations included "strong buy," "buy," "hold," and "sell." Well, where would an investor be without professional help like that?

We suppose others may have their own reasons to invest in stocks, but we invest for capital appreciation; we're in it for the money. Thus, we must know how to value companies. We can easily measure a company's tangible asset value based on possessions such as cash and real estate. However, the bulk of a company's present value is usually derived from an estimate of future cash flows: the X Factor. To buy stocks at a discount, we must find discrepancies between a company's intrinsic value (what it is worth) and a company's price (what it sells for).

Probabilities, Formulae, and Fortune Tellers

Even though no one can accurately and consistently predict the future, all of us engage in the daily calculation of probabilities. Some calculations are simple: A short line at the bank means I'll probably be served quickly. Exceeding the speed limit slightly is less likely to result in a citation than zooming down the highway at triple-digit speeds.

Probabilities are the stuff of everyday life, and they are inseparable from investing decisions. Estimating the value of future cash flows—in today's dollars—helps determine whether a stock is a bargain. But the future is little more than a sum of probabilities, so we must continually monitor all important factors.

Discounted Cash Flow Analysis

Professional investors commonly use the valuation method known as *discounted cash-flow analysis* to estimate the "fair market value" of a company. This analysis stems from the idea that a company's value is equal to all of the cash it could make available to investors in the future. The "discount" part of the equation reflects the idea that a dollar today is worth more than a dollar tomorrow. Thus, investors must estimate how much cash a company will generate in the future, and then estimate a fair price for that value today compared to the returns of other investments.

Projecting cash flow is complicated and depends on many variables, which themselves depend on a boatload of assumptions, including the historical performance of similar companies; the likelihood of lawsuits; competitive pressures; inflation; currency fluctuation; and other possible, probable, and unpredictable circumstances. A mistaken assumption severely distorts the calculation over time.

Compare this process to the experience of looking through a telescope. At first, far-off objects appear small and blurry, so we increase the magnification and adjust the focus to see them more clearly. But then, the slightest bump or twist of the focusing knob causes us to lose sight of our target because of the distances and magnification involved.

Such repercussions shake the stock market every quarter, when a company misses earnings-per-share forecasts by one or two pennies. Because those pennies are early factors in an equation that multiplies over years, they significantly skew an analyst's projections of the X Factor—future cash flows—and dramatically devalue today's stock price. Sometimes this is appropriate. Sometimes it is merely an overreaction based on faulty initial assumptions.

Ask investors who held shares of Whole Foods on November 3, 2006. On November 2, the company issued a press release detailing performance:

"In fiscal 2006, we produced strong operating results, reporting our third consecutive year of double-digit comparable store sales growth, an increase in adjusted diluted earnings per share to $1.39, and a $39 million improvement in EVA," said John Mackey, chairman, chief executive officer, and cofounder of Whole Foods Market. "We returned $358 million in cash dividends to our shareholders and are pleased to announce today a 20 percent increase in our quarterly dividend to $0.18 per share."[1]

That sounded pretty good, but the release also included this comment about the 2007 fiscal year:

> After producing such strong growth over the last three years, we believe fiscal 2007 will be a transition year for us. As we revert back to our historical comparable store sales growth range, without yet producing a fully offsetting increase in sales from new stores, we believe our total sales growth will be impacted. However, having opened six new stores over the last two months, we believe we are just beginning to execute on delivering an acceleration in store openings that will be a driver of strong sales and comps in the not-so-distant future. We remain confident in our ability to achieve our goal of reaching $12 billion in sales in fiscal 2010.

On Wall Street, "transition year" is apparently code for "abandon ship," because the stock price dropped by over 20 percent on the following day.

Intrinsic Value

Value is a topic for philosophers as well as investors; the word carries many shades of meaning. As we said above, "intrinsic value" simply refers to what we believe a company is worth, based on its net tangible assets and our estimate of today's value of its future cash flows. (See Chapter 23 for a more comprehensive look at intrinsic value.) In a perfectly efficient market, stock prices reflect this intrinsic value. However, temporary inefficiencies produce discounts or premium pricing. Since the market always moves toward efficiency, over time a stock price tends to move toward an accurate reflection of intrinsic value. This is why we welcome volatility; it creates bargains, as well as opportunities to sell at a premium.

Like investing itself, determining intrinsic value is more art than science. Warren Buffett talks about intrinsic value often, but has never revealed his calculation method. Frankly, we doubt that *calculation* is the right word. *Judgment* seems more appropriate.

As a starting point, one can compare the earnings yield of a stock to that of "safer" investment options, such as Treasury bonds. For example, if a company under consideration boasts earnings-per-share of $2 and sells for $20 per share, it has an earnings yield of 10 percent ($2 / $20 = 10 percent). *(Caveat: Keep in mind what we said before about how easily "earnings" can be manipulated, and make sure to reconcile reported earnings with the cash-flow statement.)*

If 10-year Treasury bonds are paying 5 percent, the stock with a 10 percent yield may be trading at a discount. If the company has strong competitive advantage, some level of inflation protection, and good growth prospects, the stock is probably safer and more lucrative than Treasury bonds. This type of calculation is easily done on the back of a cocktail napkin, and we believe it is an excellent way to quickly compare investment opportunities of all sorts.

Valuation and Evaluation

A large and well-known consulting firm that recommends investment advisers to institutions recently told West Coast Asset Management that we were the first firm they interviewed that seriously weighs company culture when researching a prospective stock purchase. Indeed, we compile a long list of considerations that must be evaluated and relegated to either the "pro" or "con" side of the ledger. Some of this information is gathered during visits to company facilities. Other investors might sometimes meet with executives at conferences, but we believe one can benefit from kicking the tires at a company's headquarters and meeting coworkers and customers.

Evaluation is as important as valuation because thousands of interconnected factors, some intangible and others quite measurable, determine the value of a company. How do contingent liabilities such as pending lawsuits affect the future cash flows? What about pension shortfalls? Are we considering a company that has to reinvent itself regularly, such as Apple, or a company like Wrigley, that has barely changed a thing in 100 years? Which of those two faces a riskier future?

We use our experience and education to refine the assumptions that feed our equations because we're not just trying to determine the growth prospects of the company, but also how much we are willing to pay for that growth.

Remember the Point of the Exercise

Ultimately, we're looking for simple inefficiencies in the market pricing of stocks. The slam dunks appear when the hungry herd on Wall Street lets emotion overcome logic, or simply chooses to overlook a boring company. A good example during the summer of 2006 was a longtime favorite of ours, Johnson & Johnson, a strong company whose earnings yield has exceeded Treasury bond yields for the past four years. Here was a company with $18 billion in net cash, great culture, and excellent growth prospects, trading at multiples well below the market average. One of a mere handful of companies that still earns a AAA credit rating from Standard & Poor's, it seems like JNJ's performance is so consistently good that people periodically forget about it, creating a bargain opportunity.

We seek to discover and invest in stocks at discount prices. On any given day, we might believe one company is worth 50 percent less than its current price, while another might be worth 150 percent more than its current price. We still agonize over our relative confidence in the assumptions driving those numbers and the role every investment would play in our overall asset allocation.

Does a particular level of discount trigger an automatic buy? Not always. Probabilities and comparisons are in constant flux. The decision whether to buy or sell a stock depends on the opportunity cost of our current investments: Knowing what we know, is there a better place for our money right now? We cannot answer that question until we understand the present value of future cash flows: the X Factor.

Estimating the present value of future cash flows turns out to be the easy part, simply discounting future cash flows by an investor's required rate of return.

Unfortunately, the whole exercise depends on a huge assumption: the actual future cash flow! We have little confidence in projections for companies in highly competitive and frequently disruptive fields, including most technology companies. Consumer technology companies in particular, like Apple Computer (AAPL), must constantly

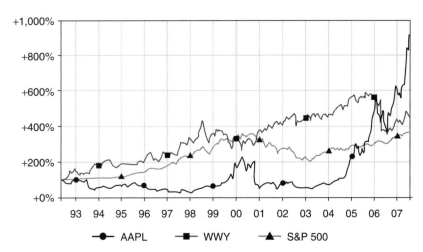

Figure 21.1 **Future Cash-Flow Probabilities**

Data Source: FT Interactive Data via Capital IQ, a division of Standard & Poor's.

reinvent their products and lower their prices. Apple is a great company that has enjoyed many successes, but who can say what Apple will be doing in 2010? (See Figure 21.1.)

However, we're more confident about what Wrigley (WWY) will be doing in 2010. And 2050. This simple business carries tremendous competitive momentum into the future because of what Berkshire Hathaway's Charlie Munger describes as an "informational advantage":

> If I go to some remote place, I may see Wrigley chewing gum alongside Glotz's chewing gum. Well, I know that Wrigley is a satisfactory product, whereas I don't know anything about Glotz's. So if one is 40 cents and the other is 30 cents, am I going to take something I don't know and put it in my mouth, which is a pretty personal place, after all, for a lousy dime?[2]

22

The Long View, and Why Women Are Better Investors

Many people sell their winners and keep their losers, hoping to capture profits quickly and recoup their losses over time. Research shows that it rarely happens, and that the winning stocks often perform even better after they are sold, while the losers continue to languish. We continuously monitor the laggards in our portfolio and determine whether to buy more or sell (to take the tax loss against future gains). Losing money hurts, so it is important to look at one's portfolio objectively, without letting pride get in the way.

If a poor-performing stock in our portfolio is undervalued, we might consider selling and then buying it back 31 days later to comply with the wash sale rule. Otherwise, we will take our losses and move on to better opportunities.

It is very easy to take short-term profits on winning stocks while avoiding selling the losers, but this strategy can ultimately lead to failure. Too many people refuse to sell their losing stocks, hoping that if they wait long enough they might get their money back. This is a big mistake, and the earlier investors realize this, the more money they can move to better investments.

Investors are also reluctant to buy a stock that has gone up in the recent past, thinking, *I should have bought more while I had the chance*, or *If only I had looked at the company six months ago*. This is a mistake, and it can easily be seen by looking at a long-term chart of companies like Wrigley or Johnson & Johnson. Stock selection should be based on the intrinsic value of a company, not on how the market behaves on any given day.

Sell, Sell, Sell

In 1998, University of California finance professor Terrance Odean published a study in the *Journal of Finance* titled "Are Investors Reluctant to Realize Their Losses?"[1] Odean studied the trading records of 10,000 investors and found that they were significantly more likely to sell winners than they were to get rid of losers. That strategy turned out to be a failure as the stocks they sold posted much bigger gains during the following year than the stocks the investors continued to hold.

Researchers have also discovered a tendency known as the *endowment effect*, in which investors place an unrealistically high value on things that they already own. An example of this would be an investor who demands $25 a share for his ownership in ABC Company, even though he is unwilling to buy the same stock at its recent price of $15.

Cutting the Weeds to Let the Flowers Bloom

As the year winds down, people evaluate tax situations and stock portfolios. Human nature leads many of us to cut the flowers in our portfolios (selling winners) and keep the weeds, instead of cutting the weeds and letting the flowers bloom.

Investing is similar to poker, in that you are constantly dealt new cards, giving you the opportunity to adjust your hand. Don't get us wrong, we are not prone to frequent trading in and out of stocks. But if you are dealt two aces and three useless cards, what are you going to do? Adjust your hand! Investing is different from poker in that you have the advantage of choosing the cards you are dealt and drawing as many times as you need. Ideally, you will get the hand you want on your first draw, but sometimes there are better opportunities down the road.

Philip Fisher's rationale for selling, from his classic *Common Stocks, Uncommon Profits* (Harper Brothers, 1958), states that one should sell:

- When it becomes clear that the original rationale for purchasing was flawed.
- When a company no longer qualifies as a top performer.
- When there is a better place to put your money.

Additionally, West Coast Asset Management will generally sell a stock if:

- A company becomes overvalued.
- Management is unsatisfactory.
- The tax loss opportunity makes sense.

If you are like most people, you probably have a mixed bag of winners and losers in your portfolio. By selling the losers, Uncle Sam lets you offset your capital gains and deduct a small amount from your taxable income, carrying forward the remaining balance.

Profits from stocks held less than one year are considered income, while profits from stocks held for more than one year are considered capital gains. Taxes on capital gains are usually much lower than taxes on short-term gains (depending on one's tax bracket and the current set of laws), so in most cases it makes sense to hold on to your appreciating stocks for at least one year. Taking a short-term gain in a taxable account is like selling the stock at a huge discount (again, depending on one's tax bracket).

If you own a stock that you know is a winner, but for one reason or another it has depreciated since you bought it, then the wash sale rule permits you to buy the stock back 31 days after selling it, while maintaining the tax loss. The risk here is that the stock could realize its intrinsic value during that 31-day period, and you would miss the boat. But the benefit of taking a loss on losers usually outweighs the consequences of desperately hanging onto them. Naturally, if they are great companies that are mere victims of circumstance, one could take advantage of the discount to buy more. Only an investor with a long-term point of view would be able to see this.

Bristol-Myers Squibb (BMY) has fallen, but can it get back up? (See Figure 22.1.) We imagine so, but wonder how long people will wait. Too many people hold on to a troubled stock in the hope that it will rebound, rather than analyzing the opportunity cost. Always ask, "Is there a better place for my money?" If you're paying attention, there usually is. Note that Johnson & Johnson's (JNJ) share price experiences periodic drops, but quickly recovers. BMY's problems continue; the company fired CEO Peter Dolan in September 2006.

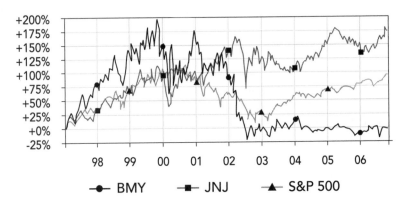

Figure 22.1 Some Are Still Waiting for the Turnaround

Data Source: FT Interactive Data via Capital IQ, a division of Standard & Poor's.

Fads and Trends

The long-term view helps entrepreneurial investors understand the context of their investments. The difference between a fad and a trend, for example, could also be the difference between sudden losses and steady gains in the stock market. The hula hoop was a fad, but its success signaled a new trend in the 1950s: a vast generation of baby boomers with leisure time and disposable income. What will that generation buy today? Tomorrow?

We follow trends to guide our investment choices, but we avoid fads like poison. Fads tend to benefit very few people—usually the fad's creator and a handful of astute investors. And here's the bad news for half of you: If you are a man, you are not as astute as you think you are.

Why Women Are Better Investors

In their outstanding paper, "Boys Will Be Boys: Gender, Overconfidence, and Common Stock Investment," Brad Barber and Terrance Odean of the University of California demonstrate that men trade stocks more frequently than women, realizing lower gains as a result.[2]

The three most important conclusions of the study, which analyzed 35,000 brokerage accounts over a six-year period, are that excessive trading lowers returns, that men trade more often than women and thus experience lower returns, and that overconfidence is the reason. Men carry an inflated sense of their own ability in financial matters. "They overestimate the probability that their personal assessments of the security's value are more accurate than the assessments of others."

Reviewing the paper, a female associate assured us she didn't need 37 pages of spreadsheets to prove what she already knew: women are more patient in deliberation and are not afraid of commitment. They choose stocks carefully and hold them longer. We mention this study not only to spice up your dinner table conversation, but also to point out that fads are distractions that cause excessive trading, while trends allow us to make solid long-term decisions. Regardless of gender, excessive trading increases fees and taxes, lowering returns!

Puka Shells and Computers

In the mid-1970s, a colleague of ours spent his high school evenings working behind the jewelry counter of a southern California Kmart store. He saw two wonders enter his glass cases: puka shell necklaces and four-function calculators. The necklaces sold for about $20 a strand, and he could barely keep them in stock. The calculators sold for $129 and moved slowly.

Within a year, calculators in a variety of sizes and styles were selling briskly for prices between $29.95 and $89.95, while puka shell necklaces were piled high on aisle display racks in the hopes they would be stolen. They weren't stolen, however, because by that time people showed no interest in wearing them.

Our friend saw for himself the difference between a trend and a fad. A fad is usually driven by changes of taste and lacks genuine lasting value. A trend, however, is generally tied to large-scale demographic shifts that can be discerned and measured.

In hindsight, that calculator was part of a productivity trend that led to desktop computers and office superstores and the resurgence in American entrepreneurship. The productivity trend, aided by technology, led to many nontechnology investment opportunities, including Federal Express and American Express.

Fads produce a product life cycle that looks like a dunce cap, and appropriately so. The trend product, whether puka shell necklaces or Razor scooters, quickly ascends and quickly descends, spending very little time in the profit zone. When we view a trend, however, we see a series of overlapping product life cycles, with one product, for example, a calculator, declining as the next product, a microcomputer, ascends. Social and demographic trends create the opportunity for multiple profitable products over a long period of time.

Many retailers are in the fad business, and often gamble an entire year's profits on one hot Christmas toy or one designer's fall collection. Other retailers, such as Guitar Center (GTRC) and Sharper Image (SHRP), capitalize on niche passions that can be fed over time with multiple fads or new technology, but how reliably, and for how long? Most retailers are simply too dependent on fashion or taste to meet our long-view investment criteria.

Icons: Products So Powerful We Take Them for Granted

Some products are so completely ingrained in the culture that we consider them a natural part of everyday life. Can you remember when Wrigley's gum was not available at the grocery checkout counter? Can you imagine a time when it will not be?

During the roaring nineties (that's 1890s!), the American trend toward more leisure, more disposable income, and more self-indulgence launched products such as Coca-Cola and Wrigley's chewing gum. Aside from the introduction of sugarless varieties 30 years ago, Coke and Wrigley enjoy the benefits of simplicity in their business; they never have to reinvent themselves (as Coke learned the hard way), and the developing world population provides their sales growth. Few companies achieve this status, moving beyond trend to icon.

Of course, even trends do not last forever, and Coca-Cola may face considerable challenges over the coming years as demand for sugary soft drinks weakens in favor of more healthful beverages.

Projections Are Not Predictions

Futurist David Zach points out that predicting trends is not as simple as projecting short-term growth rates over a longer term. For example, the increase in law school admissions in the late 1970s projected that, by 1999, three quarters of the U.S. population would be attorneys. The other quarter would be Elvis impersonators. And yes, they would all be wearing puka shell necklaces. Clearly, statistical projections cannot account for everything.

Demographics Are More Important than Psychographics

Real trends can be mapped against real numbers. That doesn't mean they are foolproof; life is unpredictable. But large-scale demographic trends point us in the right direction for picking stocks. Today, we're especially interested in age, population centers, and international politics. Psychographics, such as lifestyle and buying habits, cannot be ignored, but are less useful for our purposes. Let's look at some broad examples of demographic trends.

Aging Populations Need More Medical Care

In general, we know that the population is aging. Not only are there more people over 65 years of age, but they are wealthier than previous generations and live much longer. The leading edge of the baby boomer generation has just turned 60; in the next 20 years the average age in the United States will shift dramatically.

Common sense suggests that aging populations in wealthy countries will create a windfall for health care companies. Thanks to advances in nutrition and hygiene, people are generally healthier, but we are also more obsessed with quality of life and will spend our money freely for more energy, vitality, and time. Which health care companies can provide these benefits and do so profitably?

Population, Politics, and International Tension

Another important trend we're watching is the growth of China. The sociopolitical differences between East and West are intensified because one quarter of the world's population is concentrated in a country still viewed with suspicion by American politicians. Recent tensions, exacerbated by increasing competition for unreliable supplies of oil, suggest that defense-related stocks will still be growing for some time to come, even if we wish it were not true.

China's selection to host the 2008 Olympics raises interesting questions. Certainly, China intends to become a more significant player in world politics and culture, but when will it become easier for foreign companies to do business there? Any liberalization of economic policies in what is potentially the world's largest consumer market would certainly reverberate throughout the stock markets. Already entrenched companies like Coca-Cola would face new competition, but could also leverage their market experience to great advantage.

Spotting a Trend Narrows the Field

With the number of stocks and industries available, we are cautious but vigilant in our study of trends. It's not much of a leap to divine that health care and the defense industry may prosper because of current political, social, and demographic trends. But how many health care companies are there? How many are in direct competition with one another? Ditto for defense.

Trend watching helps us narrow down the field, but we still need to evaluate complexity, valuation, competitive advantage, and management talent to find the right companies for long-term investment.

Retailers are notoriously dependent on fads and fashions, and thus can be quite volatile (see Figure 22.2). Note that clothing retailer The Gap (GSP) has had trouble regaining the glory of its turn-of-the-century fashionableness. Macy's (M), which carries a

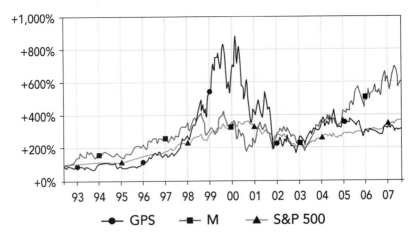

Figure 22.2   Fashion, Fads, Trends, and Time
Data Source: FT Interactive Data, via Capital IQ, a division of Standard & Poor's.

wider selection of merchandise, has managed to outperform the clothing retailer and the general market over this time frame.

Even though pharmaceutical companies like Bristol-Myers Squibb and Pfizer have had their own problems lately, pharmaceuticals in general stand to benefit from the long-term trend of aging populations in wealthy nations. Likewise, oil and gas companies sell a scarce resource to energy-hungry, growing populations. These large-scale demographic trends improve the probability that a well-run pharmaceutical or oil company will be very profitable over time. A clothing store's profitability, however, might depend largely on what Paris Hilton is seen wearing (or not wearing) at a party.

CHAPTER 23

Intrinsic Value: Putting It All Together

Throughout this book we have touched on many elements that combine to make up a company's *intrinsic value*. The term simply means, "What is the company really worth?" Unfortunately, there is no simple answer. Here is Warren Buffett's definition of intrinsic value in Berkshire Hathaway's "Owner's Manual":

> Intrinsic value can be defined simply: It is the discounted value of the cash that can be taken out of a business during its remaining life. The calculation of intrinsic value, though, is not so simple. As our definition suggests, intrinsic value is an estimate rather than a precise figure, and it is additionally an estimate that must be changed if interest rates move or forecasts of future cash flows are revised. Two people looking at the same set of facts, moreover—and this would apply even to Charlie and me—will almost inevitably come up with at least slightly different intrinsic value figures.[1]

While there is no question in our minds that buying companies at a discount to intrinsic value is the ultimate key to making money on Wall Street, estimating intrinsic value presents the greatest execution of the art, science and business of value investing. Differing opinions and assumptions about the future add up to a wide range of perceptions, analyst ratings, and price targets for individual companies on Wall Street. As entrepreneurial investors, the fewer assumptions we need to make, and the higher our convictions for a particular business, the more comfortable we can be with our estimation.

We view intrinsic value as a mosaic or jigsaw puzzle of sorts, which we assemble by assessing four key pieces: margin of safety, underlying cash flow, management quality, and new growth prospects.

Margin of Safety

The term *margin of safety* was coined by the father of value investing, Benjamin Graham. It is a concept of capital protection, in which an investor minimizes downside risk by purchasing securities when the market price is significantly below its intrinsic value.

While value investors typically view margin of safety as a discount to the present value of a business's future cash flows, we also focus on tangible assets, net of debt, which could be monetized without affecting the underlying business. *Hard assets,* such as land, buildings, cash, and marketable securities are relatively easy to value, and they provide real value and a safety cushion in case a business deteriorates or an investor makes flawed assumptions elsewhere.

For example, if XYZ Corporation is a small business with all of its eggs in one basket, an investor will have peace of mind if the company holds a large net cash balance and owns its real estate outright. By the same token, if XYZ is a very safe and profitable company with a significant amount of net tangible assets, it could return this value to shareholders in the form of share repurchases, dividends, or a value-creating acquisition. This is a common store of value that is often overlooked or underappreciated.

As risk-averse investors, the higher the margin of safety, the more comfortable we are with our assessments, and the more likely we are to make an investment. A certain degree of risk exists under any scenario, but when an investor finds an undervalued company with a high margin of safety, he or she has found an outstanding balance of security and upside potential.

Underlying Cash Flow

The present value of future cash flows generated by a company's underlying business, what we call the X Factor, is nearly always the most critical element in determining intrinsic value. And it is by far the most difficult, as it requires a number of assumptions regarding many different factors that are constantly changing.

Understanding the sustainability of a company's competitive advantage is the most crucial of these assumptions, and there are two main types to consider—cost and distinction advantage. Cost advantage is a company's ability to produce a good or service at a lower cost than its competitors, which gives it the ability to generate a higher profit margin on sales.

An example of this would be economies of scale, in which larger companies are able to lower their average cost per unit by operating on a bigger scale. For instance, Dell is able to produce computers at a lower cost than most competitors by spreading its infrastructure and fixed costs over a larger amount of production. Likewise, Wal-Mart is able to use its massive size to negotiate lower prices, which it then passes through to its customers while maintaining desired profit margins. This is known as buying power.

On the flip side, Wrigley maintains pricing power, as it has proven its ability to increase prices over time while its chewing gum has hardly changed. Dell, however, lacks pricing power, as there are a great number of computer manufacturers that continue to lower prices as technology improves and brand recognition becomes less meaningful.

Distinction advantage occurs when consumers perceive a firm's products or services as better than its competition, and will therefore pay higher prices. A great example of this would be Tiffany & Co.'s ability to consistently generate gross margins north of 50 percent.

Competitive advantages give companies an edge over rivals and an ability to create greater value over time. The stronger and more sustainable the advantages are, the more comfortable investors can be in estimating future cash flows.

Sensitivity of cash flows to interest rates, commodity prices, demographic shifts, foreign currencies, inflation, and economic cycles should be given serious consideration, as these factors can significantly impact future cash flows and their present value for the better or worse.

Once an investor is comfortable with the above factors, it is time to *measure* underlying cash flow and project what the future of the business will look like. We estimate underlying cash flow based on reported earnings adjusted for changes in working capital and special items. Changes in working capital would include increases or decreases in inventory and receivables, which should be evaluated closely if the changes are material.

Unless a business has particularly lumpy revenues, its operating cash flow should consistently exceed the amount of its reported net income. And unless a business is investing a significant amount of capital in growth initiatives, its net income should be roughly equivalent to its operating cash flow minus capital expenditures. Of course, there are always exceptions to the rule, but this is an easy way to get a rough idea of how much cash a business is truly generating. Financial statements are easily found on the Internet.

Once the cash-generating power of a business has been estimated, the degree to which it will grow or shrink must be determined by assessing many of the external factors mentioned above. From here, an investor must determine his required rate of return, which will determine how much he is willing to pay for the future cash flows today, as we explained in Chapter 21.

At the end of the day, evaluating a company's profitability is very similar to evaluating your own finances. Just follow the cash!

Management Quality

Intangibles such as management quality and alignment of interests can truly make or break an investment. By itself, insider ownership and insider buying or selling of stock on the open market does not tell the whole story of interest alignment, but in combination with an executive's history and reputation, these details shed a lot of light on the company's attitude toward shareholders.

Management either creates or destroys capital through capital allocation skills, and we look for organizations that recognize the importance of per-share value creation. One can get a good sense of management's philosophy and ability to allocate capital by evaluating executives' track record—both at the existing company and in prior roles. One can also use industry contacts to evaluate the management's reputation, and talk to coworkers to corroborate management's public persona. We like companies that are entrepreneurial and opportunistic, for example, repurchasing stock when it is cheap and divesting or acquiring businesses and assets when it is accretive to shareholders.

Although somewhat intangible and difficult to judge, management's impact must be evaluated. All else being equal, one business might be significantly more profitable with a visionary manager, while another might benefit more from a day-to-day pragmatist with a "nuts

and bolts" approach to the business. Does the management team actively seek opportunities for growth? Is it committed to a "to not do"
list that protects the company from ill-fitting acquisitions? Of course,
vision alone accomplishes little; we need leaders who know how to
execute well and generate *results*.

Management sets the tone and models the company culture.
Do coworkers take pride in the company and their work? Does the
company attract quality coworkers as a result of its culture and reputation? Do coworker incentives support per-share value? Does management remove obstacles for coworkers, or do they micromanage
and demoralize the team? You can see much of this when you walk
through the front door, if you look at the right people. It's very much
a cliché, but an effective one: We want to invest in people with fire
in their eyes.

The leaders of public companies also benefit from financial and
capital markets expertise, as well as operational expertise. A public
company faces pressures well beyond the day-to-day operation of the
business; management must recognize Wall Street's role in the company's future, managing expectations and optimizing the company's
capital structure. At the end of the day, per-share value creation is what
it is all about, so managing analyst/investor expectations and access-
ing the right types of capital at the right time are very valuable skills.

Some investors balk at large compensation packages. We do not
mind a large compensation package, so long as it is an aligned compensation package. We expect leaders to be rewarded for long-term
performance, and expect the rewards to be commensurate with their
achievements. In other words, as shareholders, we want to pay them
well for paying us well.

Finally, we must assess the independence and quality of the board
of directors. Do they understand shareholder value creation? Are
they actively involved and knowledgeable about the business?

New Growth Prospects

Identifying and evaluating new growth prospects contributes much
to an entrepreneurial investor's success. This is a three-step process:
(1) Identify new growth prospects or catalytic events; (2) determine
the likelihood of success; (3) estimate the value if successful. Naturally, we seek opportunities with multiple potential catalysts and
higher levels of potential value creation.

Ideally, one finds a company trading at a significant discount to the value of its existing business and assets, with multiple potential catalysts that are likely to become company-changing events. This enables a portfolio to significantly outperform the market during down and up years. We call this *option value.*

Potential catalysts could include the following:

- New drug or medical device approval.
- New oil or natural gas discovery.
- Evaluation of strategic alternatives.
- Divestment of nonstrategic assets.
- Sale of the entire company.
- Share repurchase.
- Special dividend.
- Spin-off of nonsynergistic business.
- Share structure unification.
- Activist shareholder.

Solving the Puzzle

Think about the methodical way we learn to complete a jigsaw puzzle. First, we turn all the pieces right side up so we can see them clearly. Then we separate the edge pieces and build the frame, filling in the details piece by piece. At all times, we keep the reference picture in sight.

Similarly, we know what an outstanding potential investment looks like: It features a high margin of safety and is cheap, based on underlying cash flow, quality management, and new growth prospects. When we believe these basic pieces exist, we fill in as many details as possible, always referring back to our ideal picture. With enough experience, one can put the puzzle together fairly quickly; or more to the point, one can toss the puzzle aside quickly when it becomes clear that pieces are missing (see Figure 23.1).

An entrepreneurial investor must have a practical methodology for estimating intrinsic value; it is the only way to know whether a good company is available at a discount. And buying good companies at a discount is the path to wealth in the stock market.

As Warren Buffett has said, "Price is what you pay; value is what you get." Is estimating the intrinsic value of a company the most important component of entrepreneurial investing? It very likely

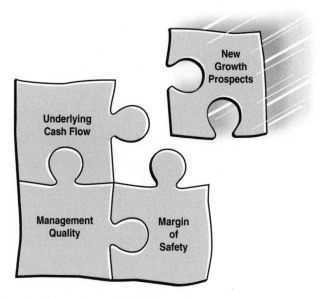

Figure 23.1   More than the Sum of Its Parts

is, because until you know "what you get," you cannot know what to pay. And what you pay ultimately determines the success of your investments.

CHAPTER
24

Inspirational Figures: Howard Hughes

Istory offers many examples of heirs to large fortunes who, through laziness, incompetence, or low character, managed to squander their forebears' inheritance and die penniless. Others, however, take the gifts bestowed upon them and use them to build something greater, and something of their own. Despite many obstacles and inner demons, Howard Hughes fought his way into the latter category.

Miramax Films' *The Aviator*[1] reminds us that Howard Hughes was a national hero before his image devolved into a caricature of mental illness and eccentricity. And although Hughes was sometimes a poor businessman, his life illustrates three principles of value to anyone seeking his own fortune:

1. Income from intellectual property can fuel other dreams.
2. Passion ignites a dream, but hard work and commitment make it real.
3. Money isn't everything.

John D. Rockefeller, the richest American ever, said, "Mere money-making has never been my goal; I had an ambition to build." Hughes also had ambition to build, to create, and to achieve. We feel his life story provides valuable lessons for the youth of today, who seem addicted to instant gratification, according to noted pediatrician and author Mel Levine.[2]

Levine's book, *Ready or Not, Here Life Comes* (Simon & Schuster, 1995), is a study of 20-somethings, whose cultural ethos seems to revolve around a "no worries" lifestyle. No worries, no plans, no responsibility, no direction. Thus, we see an epidemic of people nearing 30 but living with their parents, wondering what to do when they grow up. Hughes's story presents a stark contrast. Thrust into adulthood at the age of 18, he forged ahead, achieved great things, and never looked back.

Greatness Thrust upon Him

But for fate, Hughes might have taken the easy road; he was a terrible student, bouncing from private school to private school without a care in the world. But when he was just 17, his mother died from complications of minor surgery, and he lost his father to a heart attack less than two years later. Still a teenager, Hughes suddenly assumed responsibility for a great fortune and the business that created it.

Hughes's wealth sprang from his father's invention, a 166-edged rotary drill bit that made it possible to drill for oil through thick rock formations. The Hughes Tool Company leased the drill bit to oil companies, and controlled all revenues derived from the design. Just as America was becoming dependent on automobiles, America's oil industry became dependent on the Hughes drill bit. This invention financed nearly all of Hughes's many adventures in film and aviation.

By 1924, at the age of 19, Hughes acquired complete control of Hughes Tool Company, but rather than devote himself full time to the company, he chose to explore other options. In 1925, Hughes relocated to California.

Oscar and Howard

Hughes's experience in Hollywood mirrors a frequent pattern in his life story: He took an interest in filmmaking; his interest turned to obsession, and with obsession came a desire for control. First, he financed a couple of silent comedies, one of which won an Academy Award for its director, Lewis Milestone.

Encouraged, Hughes sought greater success and began work on a film about the Royal Air Force in World War I. But the neophyte filmmaker was not content to merely finance *Hell's Angels*; he wrote and directed the film himself, and assembled the largest private air force in the world. Moreover, he indulged another new interest by piloting one of the planes himself, against the advice of his hired stunt pilots.

Thus, Hughes experienced the first of three major plane crashes. After a few weeks of recuperation, he was back at work. However, talking pictures had by this time asserted their dominance in Hollywood, so Hughes reshot nearly all of *Hell's Angels* with a new actress, blonde bombshell Jean Harlow.

Hughes's perfectionism delayed release of the film for years; when it finally debuted in 1930, it was a huge success. Unfortunately, the film had cost so much to make ($4 million) that it lost money, despite setting box office records. He continued to produce films, and eventually bought RKO Pictures, but by the early 1930s his interest in aviation had eclipsed his desire to make movies.

Setting Records, Setting Bones

In the 1930s, Howard Hughes held nearly every important speed record for flying. First, Hughes bought and redesigned a small Army Air Corps racer. The hangar and small crew he hired to work on the plane eventually became the Hughes Aircraft Company, one of the country's largest defense contractors.

Hughes took an active role in designing and testing airplanes, and once again nearly lost his life. While testing the company's XF-11 photoreconnaissance plane in 1946, Hughes crashed and was critically injured. Nevertheless, he once again took the role of test pilot on a newer version of the same plane less than a year later. But injuries from the crash resulted in a prescription for, and eventual addiction to, codeine.

Although the XF-11 and Hughes's troop carrier plane (popularly known as the Spruce Goose) were not completed in time for World War II, the Hughes companies did contribute many armament innovations to the war effort.

Moreover, Hughes's companies played a huge role in space exploration and commerce: According to the Howard Hughes Corporation Web site, "The 1965 Hughes Early Bird was the first communications satellite ever launched for commercial use. And in 1966, the first soft landing on the moon was made by the Hughes *Surveyor* spacecraft."

More than just a filmmaker, pilot, and designer, Hughes the visionary acquired controlling interests in several airlines, including Trans World Airlines (TWA), and Air West Airlines.

Legal Challenges and Cash Windfalls

Although known as a flamboyant millionaire and Hollywood playboy, Hughes was a very shy youngster, and that description was probably closest to his true nature. The cutthroat and duplicitous realms of politics and defense contracting were a poor fit for a dreamer like Hughes, who always questioned authority and strove to set his own course.

To compete at the highest level, Hughes associated with many people of dubious character, including former spies and FBI agents, muckraking journalists, reputed mobsters, and United States congressmen. He found himself embroiled in controversy as a Senate committee investigated Hughes for not delivering two planes contracted by the government.

Some people maintain the investigation was a smear campaign arranged by the owner of Pan American Airlines, himself a visionary businessman who practically invented the modern airline industry. Others say that Hughes was simply being held accountable for wasting $40 million of government money. Perhaps no one will ever know all the details, but Hughes certainly sank to the level of the lowest common denominator in Washington, using cash "loans" and other incentives to influence tax policy and other legislation that might impact his business interests.

In their book *Empire: The Life, Legend and Madness of Howard Hughes* (W. W. Norton & Company, 1981), Donald L. Bartlett and James B. Steele write, "In 1966 he was forced to sell his TWA shares after losing a lawsuit that charged him with illegally using the airline to finance other investments. The sale netted Hughes over half a billion dollars. To many, it seemed more like a victory than a defeat."[3]

Indeed, Hughes had always been willing to leverage his holdings, from the Tool Company to the studios to the airlines, to finance bigger and bolder dreams. He was a risk taker, which led to many great victories and many crushing defeats. And although TWA executives criticized his erratic, detached, and impulsive management style, the company (and the airline industry itself) fared no better after his departure. In the aftermath of the TWA sale, he found himself with half a billion dollars, few friends, and a desire to be alone.

Real Estate and Real Enough Demons

Increasingly dependent on drugs and disenchanted with business, politics, and Hollywood, Hughes took up residence at the Desert Inn Hotel in Las Vegas. At the time, Las Vegas was in a slump. When the Desert Inn decided they could make more money renting out Hughes's floor to tourists, they tried to evict him. He responded by buying the hotel.

Then he bought more hotels and casinos in Las Vegas, Reno, and the Bahamas. Former FBI agent Robert Maheu oversaw Hughes's business interests in Las Vegas, and defended his employer's approach: "When he came here, he wanted to tie up all the property on the Strip to develop it properly. He didn't want it to be honky-tonk or Coney Island. Hughes was a catalyst in the city cleaning up its act."

Hughes expanded his real estate holdings, bought gold and silver mines, and media outlets, establishing the Hughes Sports Network. But even as his business interests were revitalized, Hughes himself was sinking further into paranoia and drug abuse. During the last years of his life, Hughes took up residence in the Bahamas and Mexico, presumably for easier access to codeine. When he died in 1976, he had not been seen publicly or photographed in 20 years.

The Aviator: Redemption of a Legacy

At the end, Hughes's apparent mental illness and drug addiction overshadowed his lifetime of daring achievements in the public consciousness. But as we noted at the outset, he was a genuine American hero before he came to be portrayed as a lunatic. Defenders point out that his behavior did not significantly deteriorate until after his third plane crash and surely was exacerbated by the pain medication required at that time.

To his credit, Hughes was always himself, carving his own path in life and doing things his own way. His life's example calls to mind a great quotation of Henry David Thoreau: ". . . if one advances confidently in the direction of his dreams, and endeavors to live the life which he has imagined, he will meet with a success unexpected in common hours."

Hughes had more than vision; he had commitment to his vision. Consider that World War II was over before he completed his unique wooden troop-carrying airplane, nicknamed the Spruce Goose.

Nevertheless, Hughes finished the plane and flew it himself. Great respect is owed a man who finishes what he starts.

Rather than enjoy the leisure available to him as a teenager, Hughes leveraged his fortune to pursue great dreams, many of which he saw to fruition through personal sacrifice and long hours of hard work. One after another, he set goals and steadfastly achieved them, in filmmaking, aviation, and real estate, creating a legacy of businesses that fueled the southern California and Nevada economies long after his death.

The story of Howard Hughes reminds us that illness can befall anyone, and that no matter how much fortune or fame we achieve, there are far more important things in life. But his story also shows us the power of passion, about making a choice, giving it your all, and finding uncommon success.

Epilogue

THE FORTUNE COOKIE THAT ATE WALL STREET

Your eyes believe what they see. Your ears believe others. Why are we so obsessed with this fortune cookie wisdom? Successful investing is sometimes a matter of learning who you can trust. Think of this book as a crash course in learning how to trust yourself to select good investments and avoid bad ones. You know more about investing than you think you do, and our goal is to help you trust your eyes more and your ears a little less. Let's review the key points of the book from this perspective.

Part 1: Think like an Owner: The Art of the Entrepreneurial Investor

Eyes, Ears, and Common Sense. It will take Wall Street analysts weeks, months, or years to appreciate what you can see today in your own business or daily life.

Cool Heads Prevail. To paraphrase Warren Buffett, we can benefit from other people's folly. When the gamblers, speculators, and amateurs panic, investors scoop up the bargains.

Understand What You Own. Simple companies are easier to evaluate and monitor. In any case, stay within your circle of competence.

Concentrate Your Portfolio. A portfolio of 10 to 15 stocks can mitigate unsystematic risk, while creating a better opportunity for each company to impact overall performance.

Just Buy the Best. Invest in individual companies rather than large funds or "categories" of stocks. Seek out the best opportunities—companies selling at a discount to their intrinsic value.

In general, mutual funds underperform when compared to concentrated portfolios.

Benjamin Graham. The father of value investing reminds us that "investing is most intelligent when it is most businesslike."

Part 2: Companies Worth Owning

The Big Secret of Brand Management. Brands are managed by customers, not by companies. If customers do not come first, investors won't rate highly either.

Insist on Competitive Advantage. If a company cannot instantly offer a cogent description of its competitive advantage, it has not won the right to your investment.

Account for Culture. Do not take company culture lightly. We believe it is the least appreciated, least understood success factor.

Interpret Elasticity. Don't be intimidated by the word *elasticity.* It just means that the demand for some products drops as prices rise, but not for others. Oil is relatively inelastic, and demand is rising. What do you think will happen to the price? How will it affect other prices?

Watch Out. First of all, everyone should read Peter Lynch's *One Up on Wall Street.* The chapter "Stocks I'd Avoid" offers a primer on bad investments, from "whisper stocks," to "the next something," to "diworsifications." Second, there is no such thing as one cockroach. If you see evidence of incompetence or malfeasance at a company, trust your instincts and run away.

David Packard. Some say that "only Nixon could go to China," and likewise, only an extremely practical engineer could envision a workplace that truly appreciates the value of the humans within.

Part 3: The Owner's Manual

Consider the Source. Televised investment advice is entertaining and sometimes illuminating, but only one-on-one advice can adequately consider your specific needs and goals.

Follow the Money. When reading a financial statement, pay particular attention to the cash flow and balance sheet. As the saying goes, "Rich or poor, it's good to have money."

Study the Footnotes. Annual reports hold many hidden messages. Use the footnotes, accountant's comments, and comparisons with past reports to decode the mystery.

Watch Out for Inventory. Fast-turning, liquid inventory is almost as good as cash. How a company accounts for inventory can tell you a lot about its future risks.

Consult the Checklist. A quick review of 10 specific factors can help you decide whether a company meets the entrepreneurial investing minimum criteria.

Bernard Baruch. The "park bench statesman" considered himself a speculator, but he laid much of the groundwork for entrepreneurial investing through his combination of hands-on research and opportunistic flexibility.

Part 4: What's It Worth—To *Me?*

Remember Your ABCs. Entrepreneurial investors practice a form of value investing, which seeks to buy real Assets at a Bargain price, expecting a Catalyst that will increase the price.

Wait Till the Moon Is Full. The price you pay for valuation is the prime determinant of your returns. Everyone wants to buy low and sell high, but buying low is the really tricky part. Wait until the price is right!

The X Factor. Despite the investment industry's obsession with the present value of future cash flows, all such calculations are based on a series of cascading assumptions. Some companies offer better probabilities of predictable future cash flow.

Trend toward a Long View. The profit life cycle of a fad looks like a dunce cap, and for good reason. Instead, look for demographic trends and understand which businesses are positioned to benefit from long-term social, political, and economic shifts.

Intrinsic Value: Putting It All Together. One cannot know what to pay for a company until one knows what it is really worth. Understand how margin of safety, underlying cash flow, management quality, and future growth prospects combine to comprise the true value of a company.

Howard Hughes. The tragedy of Hughes's later years should not blind people to the vision, character, and heroism of his life.

Who would have thought a fortune cookie could offer such good investing advice?

Producer, writer, and director Quentin Tarantino once attributed his success to the fact that he didn't go to film school; he went to films. He used his eyes, rather than his ears. Thus, he developed his own vision, rather than repeating the clichés of "experts." We think every investor should have his or her own vision, respect his or her personal experience, and know that few "experts" consistently beat the market.

Too many intelligent people doubt themselves and trust experts. Granted, too often the wrong people trust themselves and ignore experts. Studies show that the most incompetent people are most likely to overrate their abilities, while the most competent people tend to underrate their skills. This would be hilarious if it weren't so obviously true. Be honest with yourself, and you will see that you know more about investing than you think you do. That doesn't mean you have the time and temperament to manage your own investments, but the information in this book could also help you select a qualified investment manager who is a good fit with your own sensibilities.

Remember also that you don't have to be an entrepreneur to invest well, but you can employ entrepreneurial focus, opportunism, and involvement to improve your results. We wish you the best of fortune.

About the Authors

Kinko's founder **Paul Orfalea** launched West Coast Asset Management with Lance Helfert in 2000 as a private, independent money manager serving high-net-worth individuals, families, institutions, and charitable foundations. Paul is widely renowned for his entrepreneurial success, growing a single copy shop into the industry leader with 1,100 branches worldwide. Paul's passion for investing dates back to his early teens, when he would skip school to spend afternoons at the office of his father's stockbroker.

Fresh out of business school at the University of Southern California, Paul started Kinko's and formed a stock club for his business partners, helping them manage the income from their fast-growing stores. Growing Kinko's and his investments through the financial ups and downs of the 1970s, 1980s, and 1990s, Paul observed that the management lessons of his company were directly transferable to his investment strategies.

"Knowledge of economics helps, but it's more important to understand value and human nature. Running a business with 25,000 coworkers reinforced my belief that a company is not a collection of machines or real estate or cash or even ideas; a company is made of people. Business experience increases both your knowledge and your intuition—your sensitivity to the complexity of human affairs."

Paul's approach to value is a cornerstone of West Coast Asset Management's strategy. "If you're going to buy a house, you get to know the neighborhood and the relative value of homes there. You do your homework and you know whether the house you're looking at is a good deal or not. The more research you do, the better your odds of buying the right house. It's the same thing with stocks, but the research is more complex."

WCAM president and co-founder **Lance Helfert** developed his professional skills during his tenure with Wilshire Associates and M. L. Stern & Co., where he gained experience in the full range of financial strategies and services. At Wilshire, Lance led a team that managed an investment portfolio valued at close to $1 billion for high-net-worth individuals and institutional clients.

Lance holds a bachelor of science degree in business administration from Pepperdine University in Malibu, California. As president of WCAM, he manages business development, defines the investment policies, and serves on the investment committee with Paul and Atticus; the three of them personally approve the investment selections for WCAM.

One of the chief lessons of Lance's experience is the value of intensive research. "Portfolio concentration is essential to our philosophy, because we want to be richly rewarded when we are right. One advantage of concentration is that we thoroughly understand the businesses we invest in, which contributes to our margin of safety."

WCAM Chief Investment Officer **Atticus Lowe** is a CFA Charterholder and has completed the Value Investing Executive Education Program at Columbia University's Graduate School of Business. He is responsible for investment research and portfolio management. Honored as a member of the "Forty Under 40" Class by the *Pacific Coast Business Times*, Atticus holds a bachelor of arts degree in economics and business from Westmont College in Montecito, California. He has been interviewed in *Oil and Gas Investor* magazine and *Value Investor Insight*, and was a featured speaker at the Value Investing Congress.

Dean Zatkowsky has worked with Paul Orfalea for over 20 years, holding executive marketing positions at Kinko's and West Coast Asset Management. An operationally biased marketer, Dean believes that "to do better than the competition, you have to be better than the competition. When you offer real value to clients, the marketing tactics are trivial. Maintaining competitive advantage is the real challenge." Dean holds a bachelor of arts degree in communication studies from the University of California-Santa Barbara.

Notice and Disclosures

		Composite Assets		Annual Performance Results					
Year End	Total Firm Assets (Millions)	U.S. Dollars (Millions)	No. of Accts	Gross	Net	S&P 500	NASDAQ	DJIA	Composite Dispersion
2006	433	205	65	26.30%	25.02%	15.80%	9.52%	19.00%	1.5%
2005	335	171	83	12.24%	11.06%	4.88%	1.37%	1.94%	2.4%
2004	309	129	61	27.61%	26.47%	10.83%	8.59%	5.27%	1.90%
2003	117	80	34	26.26%	25.13%	28.66%	50.01%	28.29%	0.80%
2002	50	50	22	−4.11%	−5.04%	−22.10%	−31.53%	−15.03%	0.70%
2001*	34	34	16	3.15%	2.47%	−14.94%	−29.66%	−6.47%	

Table heading: WCAM Equity Composite

* Results shown for the year 2001 represent partial period performance from February 1, 2001 through December 31, 2001.

Table N.1.   WCAM Equity Composite Performance 2001-2006

West Coast Asset Management is a private, independent money manager serving individuals, families, trusts of all kinds, and businesses.

This material is for informational purposes only. No recommendation to purchase or sell securities is made, nor does this constitute an offer of any kind. Data were obtained from publicly available sources that we believe are reliable. West Coast Asset Management makes no warranty or representations as to the accuracy or usefulness of this information. The principals, coworkers, directors, and clients of West Coast Asset Management may or may not own shares in the companies discussed. A list of companies recently reviewed in our audio recordings, presentations, newsletters, and other publications is available on request. Prospective investors should always remember that past performance is no guarantee of future results.

Third-party trademarks and service marks are the property of their respective owners.

WCAM Equity Composite contains fully discretionary equity accounts. Prior to October 1, 2004, the composite was named the WCAM Composite. Effective October 1, 2006, the minimum account size for this composite is $500,000. Prior to October 1, 2006, the minimum was $100,000.

West Coast Asset Management, Inc. has prepared and presented this report in compliance with the Global Investment Performance Standards (GIPS®).

West Coast Asset Management, Inc. is a registered investment adviser. The firm maintains a complete list and description of composites, which is available upon request. For comparison purposes, the composite is shown against the Standard & Poor's (S&P) 500, Dow Jones Industrial Average (DJIA), and Nasdaq indices. These indices are unmanaged and represent a more diversified list of securities than that reflected in the composite. In addition, the composite may invest in securities outside of those represented in the indices shown. Additional information regarding the indices is available upon request.

Results are based on fully discretionary accounts under management, including those accounts no longer with the firm. Past performance is not indicative of future results.

The U.S. dollar is the currency used to express performance. Returns are presented gross and net of management fees and include the reinvestment of all income. Net-of-fee performance was calculated using actual management fees. The annual composite dispersion presented is an asset-weighted standard deviation calculated for the accounts in the composite the entire year. Additional information regarding policies for calculating and reporting returns is available upon request.

The management fee schedule is as follows: 1.50 percent on all assets. Actual investment advisory fees incurred by clients may vary. Composite strategy includes investments in foreign-based companies, for which performance is presented net of foreign withholding taxes on dividends, interest income, and capital gains. Withholding taxes may vary according to the investor's domicile.

The WCAM Equity Composite was created January 31, 2001. West Coast Asset Management, Inc.'s compliance with the GIPS standards has been verified for the period January 31, 2001, through December 31, 2006, by Ashland Partners & Company LLP. In addition, a performance examination was conducted on the WCAM Equity Composite beginning January 31, 2001. A copy of the verification report is available upon request.

Subscribe to the West Coast Asset Management newsletter at www.wcam.com.

Notes

Chapter 1

1. Simon Reynolds, Thoughts of Chairman Buffett: Thirty Years of Unconventional Wisdom from the Sage of Omaha; New York, Harper Collins 1998, p. 65.

Chapter 2

1. Alan Greenspan, At the Annual Dinner and Francis Boyer Lecture of The American Enterprise Institute for Public Policy Research, Washington, D.C., December 5, 1996.
2. *Men in Black* (motion picture), 1997, Amblin Entertainment.
3. Douglas Adams, *Hitchhiker's Guide to the Galaxy*, London, Pan Books, 1979.
4. Benjamin Graham, *The Intelligent Investor*, (re-issue of 1949 edition), New York, HarperBusiness Essentials, 2005.

Chapter 3

1. *Sudden Impact* (motion picture), 1983, Warner Brothers.
2. *Dirty Harry* (motion picture), 1971, Warner Brothers.
3. *Magnum Force* (motion picture), 1973, Warner Brothers.

Chapter 4

1. Warren Buffett, Berkshire Hathaway Annual Report, 1993.
2. Charlie Munger, comments at Berkshire Hathaway Annual Meeting, April 29, 2000.

Chapter 7

1. *The Thin Blue Line*, American Playhouse, 1988.

Chapter 9

1. Jeff Goodell, "Losing The HP Way," Salon.com, March 22, 2002.
2. Corporate Objectives, www.hp.com.

Chapter 10

1. *Casablanca* (motion picture), Warner Brothers Pictures, 1942.
2. *The Naked Gun* (motion picture), Paramount Pictures, 1988.

Chapter 11

1. Standard & Poor's stock report, October 31, 2006.

Chapter 13

1. Jean Chatzky, "Pick an Advisor Who Connects with You," CNNMoney.com, June 26, 2006.
2. Matthew Futterman, "Investing Advice turns into a Loud, Violent TV Show," *The Seattle Times*, October 30, 2005.

Chapter 15

1. *The Fugitive* (motion picture), Warner Brothers, 1993.
2. Matt Krantz, "How to Read an Annual Report," *USA Today*, February 24, 2004.
3. Tom Waits, *Small Change* (audio recording), Elektra, 1976.

Chapter 16

1. Joseph T. Wells, "Ghost Goods: How to Spot Phantom Inventory," *Journal of Accountancy*, June 2001.

Chapter 18

1. The inspiration and primary resource for this chapter is James Grant's Bernard Baruch: The Adventures of a Wall Street Legend, New York, John Wiley & Sons, 1997.

Chapter 19

1. Burton Malkiel, *A Random Walk Down Wall Street*, New York, W.W. Norton & Company, 2003, p. 24.
2. Bernard Baruch, *My Own Story*, Holt, Rinehart and Winston, 1957.

Chapter 20

1. Jeremy Siegal, "Beware of the 'Growth Trap,'" Yahoo! Finance, February 23, 2006.

Chapter 21

1. Press Release: Whole Foods Markets Reports Fourth Quarter Results, Whole Foods Investor Relations website, November 2, 2006.
2. Charlie Munger, "Art of Stock Picking," vinvestor.com, November 29, 2006.

Chapter 22

1. Terrance Odean, "Are Investors Reluctant to Realize Their Losses," *Journal of Finance* 53, 1998.
2. Brad Barber & Terrance Odean, "Boys will be Boys: Gender, Overconfidence, and Common Stock Investment," *The Quarterly Journal of Economics*, February 2001.

Chapter 23

1. Warren Buffett, Berkshire Hathaway Owner's Manual, January 1999.

Chapter 24

1. *The Aviator* (motion picture), Miramax Films, 2004.
2. Mel Levine, *Ready or Not, Here Life Comes*, New York, Simon & Schuster, 2005.
3. Donald L. Bartlett & James B. Steele, *Empire: the Life, Legend and Madness of Howard Hughes*, New York, W.W. Norton & Company, 1981.

Index